EMPLOYE~~X~~R
ENGAGEMENT

The fresh and dissenting voice on the
Employment Relationship

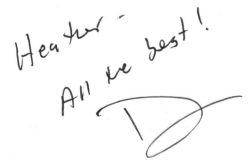

Heather –
All ~~the~~ best !

EMPLOYE~~X~~R ENGAGEMENT

The fresh and dissenting voice on the
Employment Relationship

THOMAS MAHAN
DANNY NELMS

FOREWORD BY MARSHALL GOLDSMITH

Indigo River Publishing

EmployER Engagement

© 2020 by Thomas F. Mahan and Danny A. Nelms

Editors: Dianna Graveman and Regina Cornell
Cover Design: Tim Barber
Interior Design: Nikkita Kent

Indigo River Publishing
3 West Garden Street, Ste. 718
Pensacola, FL 32502
www.indigoriverpublishing.com

Ordering Information:
Quantity sales: Special discounts are available on quantity purchas-
es by corporations, associations, and others. For details, contact the
publisher at the address above.

Orders by US trade bookstores and wholesalers: Please contact the
publisher at the address above.

Printed in the United States of America

Library of Congress Control Number: 2019954589
ISBN: (Paperback) 978-1-950906-25-3, (Hardback) 978-1-950906-26-0
(Ebook) 978-1-950906-27-7

First Edition

*With Indigo River Publishing, you can always expect great books,
strong voices, and meaningful messages.
Most importantly, you'll always find . . . words worth reading.*

"Mahan and Nelms present the reader with excellent data and sound recommendations to improve employee retention and engagement. As an HR professional, I especially appreciate the authors' recommendations to utilize turnover costs to build the necessary business case to senior officers; to have employers pilot and adopt their own best practices (rather than chase the most current HR fad); and for Operation Managers to own employee retention and engagement. *EmployER Engagement* is a must read and must follow road map for any organization genuinely interested in building a more productive workplace."

Michael F. Cassity, MA, SPHR
Division VP- Human Resources (Retired)
HCA

"*EmployER Engagement* insightfully makes the case for leaders to have the courage to connect and engage with employees. Mahan and Nelms provide excellent data to support the Employer Engagement premise and the necessary tools to build effective strategies for organizational engagement and retention. The manager who effectively connects with employees demonstrates engaging behavior, and in return so will employees. The ideas shared in this book helped me define more and better actions."

Phil Brown
Sr. Vice President, Mohawk Industries

"Mahan and Nelms vividly describe the shifting workforce dynamics and the need for employers to better engage their people. This mandate is to not only compete, but to ultimately survive. There has never been a more critical period in the war for talent."

Bob Ravener
Author, Consultant, Speaker, Board Member, Former EVP and Chief People Officer, Dollar General Corporation

"Strong, bold, and convicting with many original thoughts and ideas and some that are painfully obvious (but need to be said). Alarming in that many executives don't already get it. Motivational, quotable, and easy to follow. Right from the beginning of *EmployER Engagement*, Mahan and Nelms have knocked this out of the park."

Mike Fitzgerald
President, Fitzgerald MSI, Peak Performance Consulting
Former EVP and Chief Talent Officer, State Bank and Trust Company

"Within most businesses, there are two major costs that are rarely managed properly. One is healthcare costs which could be reduced significantly, and the other is the cost of human capital. These two talented and experienced authors have written a book that may be the absolute best source on how to do the latter. I doubt anyone has studied the topic more. They offer what I call empirical wisdom that is solid and actionable, and which has been proven repeatedly to reduce cost significantly, improve productivity and engender a state of well-being among the workforce. Some books are a good read, some are a good resource to be visited frequently. This book is both. I strongly encourage anyone trying to manage a business to buy this book. It may challenge your existing paradigms regarding leadership, employee engagement, recruiting and retention. Much of what is being taught about these topics is not true and simply does not work. If you want your organization to be a class act, staffed with highly motivated, energized people, this book will point you in the right direction."

W. Terry Howell, Ed.D.
CEO, Sky Solutions, LLC
Author: *Healthcare is Killing US: The Power of Disruptive Innovation to Create a System that Cares More and Costs Less.*

"Mahan and Nelms do an outstanding job sharing science and data in a 'common sense' way. *EmployER Engagement* validates instincts associated with engagement and retention, but pushes you to think about these constructs differently. As the business world becomes more competitive and as employment trends continue to be positive, organizations must have an even greater sense of urgency to retain their employees. *EmployER Engagement* provides excellent ideas that one can actually USE to drive change – today."

Kim Nowell, SPHR
Former Chief People Officer
Sav-A-Lot & Ingram Barge

"As a former client of Work Institute, I am fully aware of the value gained by asking employees for feedback using the approach laid out in *EmployER Engagement*. Mahan and Nelms remind us not only of the value of the right data, but the necessary steps to ensure employee feedback drives meaningful change."

Glen Maul
Managing Partner, The Maul Group Former EVP and
Cqhief People Officer, Brookdale Senior Living

"Mahan and Nelms understand the critical elements required to compete and win in the 21st century. *EmployER Engagement* provides proven and scalable recommendations for any organization actively working to create an engaged and motivated workforce."

John Maketa
Chief Revenue Officer of Caliper
Co-author of the best-selling book, *Now You're Thinking!*
and the recently published book, *Leading with Vision.*

"Mahan and Nelms draw on decades of experience in employee engagement to offer an unconventional approach to reducing turnover. In a market with increasing opportunities for employees, it is no longer productive to shame employees for their shortcomings or dazzle them with token benefits in the hope that they respond with increased engagement. Rather, the authors suggest, it is incumbent on the employer to create an environment that is favorable to employee satisfaction through careful listening and active response. Mahan and Nelms motivate this fresh approach with extensive data, then offer a road map to help employers be better listeners and, ultimately, improve firm performance through reduced turnover cost and a healthier employer/employee relationship."

Kara Smith, Ph.D.
Massey School of Business, Belmont University

"Mahan and Nelms have researched and succinctly captured principles and truths necessary to create an organization in which employees can realize their most personally important needs. Contrary to the past, this book establishes the responsibility of employee engagement rests on the shoulders of the employer and it provides strategies and tools to accomplish this responsibility. It provides perfect insight and a compelling business case for the most challenging issue facing all companies today: how to attract and retain the best talent in the relevant industry. I recommend this reading for all organization leaders."

Linda M. Meador, Ph.D.
President. Success Optics

Come, labor on!
No time for rest, till glows the western sky,
Till the long shadows o'er our pathways lie,
And glad sound comes with the setting sun,
"Well done, well done!"

—Jane Borthwick

CONTENTS

Employer Engagement
At-Risk Employers
Employees Don't Need You—You Need Them

The US Economy Is Flowing Steadily
Workforce Supply Is at a Trickle
Job Openings Continue to Rise
Worker Shortage Is Increasing
Voluntary Quits Are at Historic Highs
First-Year Employees Are at Highest Risk
We Can Know Why Employees Are Disengaged and Leaving
Turnover Costs Are Rising
Generational Mythologies Marginalize Employees
Reasons for Staying Are Different than Reasons for Leaving
Companies Must Be Engaged

Quit Depending on Others' Best Practices
Spinning with Benchmarks
Making Assumptions about Your Workforce
Ignoring Troubled and Troubling Manager Behaviors
Thinking Engagement and Retention Is a Human Resource Department Responsibility

Preoccupation with Data—*Only*
Recruiting Wrongly
Hiring Poorly
Not Rethinking Your Methods
Assuming College Prepares Students for Work
Overlooking Unethical, Fraudulent, and Behavioral Issues
Ignoring Career Development

Productivity
The Human Capital Audit
Calculate Your Cost of Turnover
Build a Business Case for Retention Management

EmployER Engagement and Retention Requires a Strategic Approach
EmployER Engagement: Your Opportunity
EmployER Engagement Principles
EmployER Engagement Foundations
EmployER Engagement Model

FOREWORD

I am thankful to be able to contribute my thoughts to *EmployER Engagement: On Becoming a Preferred Employer.* While my core area of expertise is what employees, especially leaders, can do to engage themselves, there is clear merit in evaluating and acting on all conditions that foster or impede the willingness and ability of an individual to become engaged. These conditions include the organization, the manager, the team, and the job itself.

As you well know, the topic "employee engagement" is ubiquitous. It is difficult to pick up a business newsletter, review a company website, or peruse the management literature without reading about employee engagement promises. Thousands of consultants are offering their own customized surefire methods to improve employee engagement. Companies are jumping on others' best engagement and retention practices, and billions of company dollars are spent on employee engagement initiatives.

Yet employee engagement sits near an all-time low. Companies, despite enormous spending, have little to show for their efforts. Most employee engagement promises have failed. Many companies blame this failure on employees and resort simply to whining and allowing disengagement to continue. Worse yet, some simply watch employees quit to pursue a better workplace. Some think the solution is to hire additional people, resolving turnover and absenteeism by increasing expenses through hiring more internal and external recruiters. Others just switch survey vendors to get prettier reports or are somehow seduced into being satisfied with simple and cheap passive questions, rather than understanding and acting on requirements necessary to improve engagement. Please note: I am not criticizing what employees offer in compromised studies; I genuinely value their contributions. Instead, my criticism is in what they could have said but didn't—as the survey did not allow it. Employees must be presented the opportunity to fully articulate their observations and, equally important, the organization needs full employee input to inform remediation and development plans.

I sometimes wonder why it is some think that the simple act of implementing a poorly designed survey is enough. An engagement study is not about engagement. Instead, fully caring, hearing, and understanding the full range of employee perspectives and acting on those observations is. Is it time to do something different? As referenced in my latest collaborative video book, *Engage and Grow* (www.engageandgrowglobal.com), the answer is a loud YES, "let's try and turn this ship around."

The ship certainly warrants turning. Too many organizations, perhaps lacking the courage to truly involve employees, get too wrapped up in popular employee engagement initiatives and fail to listen and act on employee observations that can guide the correct course.

Companies must care. They must care about employees and customers. They must care that the way employees are treated directly influences the way customers are treated. They must care about civility. Inappropriate behavior must be identified, and problematic individuals must either remediate or be expelled. Companies must not put up with behavior that conflicts with engagement opportunity. Leaders must care about development, their own and the development of others who choose to work with them. Caring requires courage. Leaders look in the mirror. Be willing to accept that you don't know everything. Be willing to consider the possibility that employees have something to offer in terms of how the work environment might best suit their social and occupational purposes. Too, employees must care. The preferred employer is the organization where care, performance, happiness, discretionary effort, and choosing to make a difference is a shared responsibility by leadership and employees. Organizations and employees can and must collaborate in making better, more engaging workplaces. Again, let's turn this employee engagement ship around.

Mahan and Nelms, in *EmployER Engagement*, are doing just that—charting a course to turn this big ship around. A courageous challenge to current employee engagement practices, the authors are inviting you to (1) consider current occupational market and employee preference data as a driver of organization decision-making and investment; (2) recognize and remedy failed legacy behaviors and mistakes that are daily made in trying to improve the workplace; (3) commence looking at human behavior, including engagement and retention, through a cost-benefit lens; and (4) implement a systematic discipline to engagement development, one that highlights the requirements for accurate and responsible problem identification, data collection, accountability, action, communication, and evaluation.

Do we need the information provided in the following pages? Yes, and we need people who can both courageously accept it and demonstrate a willingness to do something about it. We are presented with an opportunity to improve our lives and the lives of those who choose to work in our organizations. We can be happier at work and at home. And we can have the answers to what needs to be done. We need only to ask, listen—truly listen—hear, and act.

This is a fun and engaging read. Consider the possibility.

—Marshall Goldsmith, PhD

Marshall Goldsmith is the *New York Times* #1 best-selling author of *Triggers, Mojo,* and *What Got You Here Won't Get You There.*

PREFACE

I've always found work that needed doing. As a kid I raked leaves, shoveled heavy Chicago snow, and collected pop bottles at two cents each. I did those jobs at my convenience. My first real job was delivering papers, initially for the *Chicago Tribune*, then, following my dad's transfer, the *Indianapolis Star*. Food Giant store coupons came out on Thursdays—collection day. I can still hear it, a child answering the door and calling back, "Mom, the paperboy's at the door, collecting." Good days included a stop at Burger King on Highway 472. A quarter, a dime, and a nickel got me a cheeseburger, fries, and an orange drink. I was working for myself. I rode my bike, in cold and heat, just doing what I said I would do—delivering papers and collecting forty cents a week. I knew my route customers' names, and they knew me. It was a great gig for a kid on a bicycle.

Over the seasons, family moves and different jobs followed. I washed windows with Tommy, shoveled snow with Keith and Desi, and painted the neighbor's garage with Alan. At fifteen or sixteen, now able to work student hours, I got my worker's permit! Throughout high school and college, I pumped gas at the Madison Shell station, stocked racks at Robert Hall, washed dishes at Stouffer's, trained as a camp counselor on Long Island, and sold women's shoes at Bloomingdale's.

My late-college-and-early-professional career had me working summers as a counselor at Easter Seal Camp Merry Heart and as a night aide, teacher-counselor, and program supervisor at Lakeside in Spring Valley, New York, and at Cumberland House in Nashville, Tennessee. Upon completion of graduate school and licensing, I moved into private practice. During this time my interests led me into the corporate environment. As a behavior consultant to businesses, in my thirties and forties I worked for Prentice-Hall, Equicor/Cigna, Interim Services/Spherion, and Saratoga Institute. Much of my work included career counseling, team assimilation, succession planning, training supervisors to recognize aberrant behavior, and selection and assessment testing. I also counseled anxious and bullying managers and other troubled and troubling employees.

I have been fortunate in my career. I mostly have been privileged with exceptional experiences and mentors: Project Re-ED and Cumberland House School (Zaka Khan, Nelle Wheeler, Alice Shannon, Jeannie S. Williams, and Nicholas Hobbs) anchored me in ecological theory and taught me that competence can be learned and that communities, including work environments, are important; Teleometrics International (Jay Hall) taught me the applied value of measuring behavior before and during development; Saratoga Institute (Jac Fitzenz) taught me to cost human behavior in the workplace; and the Emerging Workforce Studies (Ray Marcy, Interim Services/Spherion Corporation) invited me to participate in groundbreaking research on the differing preferences and expectations of the workforce.

It has been fun. Sure, just like others, I've had bully bosses and struggled with transfer and career decisions. Excessive travel away from family and the anxieties of mergers and acquisitions fed worry. (Between 1990 and 2000, I worked for six different companies while remaining at the same desk.) Mostly I've struggled with compromised decisions made by supervisors dependent on antiquated policies, practices, and procedures—activities of a day gone by. In 2001, I founded the Work Institute to assess, cost, intervene, and evaluate organizational behaviors and conditions that support, enhance, or interfere with productive behavior in the workplace.

Throughout these past twenty years, I've worked alongside brilliant and caring workplace professionals, including Kelley O'Brien, Bill Barkley, Richard Nicorvo, Dean Weiland, William Mahan, Anne Powers, Danny Nelms, Katherine and Nathan Huddleston, Laura Hershenow Anselm, Kelsey McManus Trinko, Lindsay Sears, Tom Pichert, Mark McWatters, Jerry and Marjie Smith, Brantley Pierce, Chris Ashford, Glenn Spinner, Ryan Bearden, Mary Fink, Dan Elkins, Sandy Wybel, Will Solomon, and many other bright Vanderbilt, Clemson, and MTSU interns. This book is written with thanks for their contributions.

As of 2020, I have been working and observing the workplace for more than fifty years. Work, as when I was just a kid with a bicycle, is still a great gig.

—Thomas F. Mahan

I am as passionate today as I was thirty years ago about the human experience in the workplace. Like many in the HR field, I stumbled into it. As a college student looking for experience in the "corporate world" and with the advice of a neighbor, I walked into Arthur Andersen, LLP, then the largest accounting firm in the world. A day later I began an extraordinary journey.

I was a student at Georgia State University and, like most college students, did not have a clue what I wanted for a career. After a few months as a runner delivering faxes (yes, this was the late '80s), I was asked to join the recruiting department in the largest Andersen office, home to the national recruiting director. My time at Andersen exposed a kid from rural Georgia to a business world he'd not previously known. High-powered executives and demanding managers expected nothing less than perfection.

My professional HR career included progressively increased responsibilities in the bustling environments of hospitality, the unique world of direct mail marketing, the crazy business of mergers and acquisitions, and finally the leadership of HR teams in manufacturing and health care. Throughout this journey I often found myself fighting the status quo, or traditional HR practice, instead of building HR strategy and teams into business-aligned functions focused on driving business results. These last ten years at the Work Institute are where I have been able to integrate my business and HR acumen to work with many incredible companies, helping them become better employers. I have many years to continue my occupational journey, and it is hard to think of anything more rewarding than partnering with employers interested in creating preferred environments for employees.

As Dr. Mahan came up with the idea for this book, I found myself once again feeling rebellious—and perhaps a bit sad. Still today, too many companies remain trapped in overhyped and erroneous ideas about what it takes to engage and retain a workforce. Too many professionals continue to do things simply because that is the way they have always been done, or because that is the direction the crowd is walking. This book challenges us to think about engagement and retention in a different way. It is in this new approach, this EmployER Engagement approach, that I believe many will find the simple yet compelling direction they have been seeking.

Years ago, Eddie Bauer, the outdoorsman and retail giant, said, "Never confuse having a career with having a life." Our occupational and social/familial lives are integrated. As such, I am grateful to my mentors, managers, and coworkers. I am also thankful for my family. My mother and father managed to instill in my brother and me the idea that going to college was the right path, even though neither of them had gone. My wife, Dana, has been my best friend and constant companion for twenty-seven years. My son, Bryant, introduced the world of digital art to his mother and me and convinced us that art school was the right path for him. I cannot wait to see what his career has in store for him. I am additionally appreciative to my Work Institute family, who has walked with me on this path. Together we will continue to see where this fantastic journey takes us.

—Danny A. Nelms

Definitional Concerns

engage: en·gage | in-ˈgāj
> *transitive verb*: to offer (something, such as one's life or word) as backing to a cause or aim; to expose to risk for the attainment or support of some end; to entangle or entrap in or as if in a snare or bog; to attract and hold by influence or power; to bind (someone, such as oneself) to do something; to arrange to obtain the use or services of: HIRE; to hold the attention of: ENGROSS; to induce to participate
> *intransitive verb*: to pledge oneself: PROMISE; to make a guarantee; to come together and interlock

engagement: en·gage·ment | in-ˈgāj-mənt
> *noun*: an arrangement to meet or be present at a specified time and place; a job or period of employment especially as a performer; something that engages: PLEDGE; emotional involvement or commitment; the state of being in gear

disengage: dis·en·gage | dis-in-ˈgāj
> *transitive verb*: to release from something that engages or involves
> *intransitive verb*: to release or detach oneself: WITHDRAW

disengaged: dis·en·gaged | dis-in-ˈgājd
   adjective: DETACHED

employer: em·ploy·er | im-ˈplȯi-ər
   noun: one that employs or makes use of something or some-
   body; a person or company that provides a job paying wages or
   a salary to one or more people; one that hires others to perform
   a service or engage in an activity in exchange for compensation

employee: em·ploy·ee | im-plȯ(i)-ē
   noun: one employed by another usually for wages or salary and
   in a position below the executive level

preferred: pre·ferred | pri-ˈfərd
   adjective: liked better or best : used or wanted in preference to
   others; having special status or receiving special treatment or
   benefits

(from *Merriam-Webster.com Dictionary*)

Introduction

The journey to becoming a better employer and a better employee requires one to understand other people's views. Herein, you are invited to consider some of those views. Content included in this book is likely to provoke mixed emotional reactions, rational and irrational debates, and logical agreement. For some, the content may be difficult and trigger contentious reactions. For others it might validate current thinking and be quite agreeable.

Ponder your thoughts and feelings to the provided content. Reactions such as resistance, defensiveness, denial, helplessness, and hopelessness are likely to surface. Too, some might feel hope, acceptance, wanting, and joy surface. Please note the importance of your reactions.

As a learning aid, throughout the book are "Stop and Think" exercises. Perhaps they will help increase your awareness of your current perspective. As an example, consider the following:

⚠ STOP AND THINK

If you are a manager, think about your time as an employee; consider those days before you became a manager. What were your aspirations? What were your pressures and responsibilities inside the office? What were your pressures and responsibilities outside the office?

Were your aspirations and past experiences really any different from those of today's young employee? What might be done to make life just a bit easier?

If you are currently a nonmanagement employee, please attempt to look through the eyes of managers. Do their pressures and role expectations inside and outside the office differ from yours?

What might be done to make their lives just a bit easier?

EmployER Engagement includes this introductory chapter and five additional chapters. While *EmployER Engagement* is organized in a developmental learning sequence, the following summaries may provide shortcuts to prescient material currently relevant for you. Feel free to journey around the content in whatever order suits your preferences, intents, and purposes.

Chapter One is an executive summary and introduces the concept and logic for considering an EmployER Engagement belief and practice. Perhaps this content touches on your present experience and the ideas you are currently pondering.

Chapter Two builds the market case for EmployER Engagement, presenting economic and demographic data on workforce supply and demand. Economists and workforce behavior scientists have been predicting that the talent wars were going to get worse. Unemployment rates are at historic lows, jobs are being created, and worker availability is dwindling. As these three trends continue, predictions are spot on. The workforce futurists were correct in their predictions: the talent war is waging. In this chapter, you will find the compelling argument for an engaged employer model of management.

Chapter Three reviews and illustrates many of the mistakes employers are making as they attempt to solve their attraction, engagement, retention, and productivity problems. It is time to listen to your workforce, rather than depend exclusively on others' best practices. It is time to understand worker and workforce preferences, rather than live in yesterday's assumptions about dependence on employers. It is time to violate the conspiracy of politeness that exists in many companies. As inappropriate behavior is tolerated, it will continue.

Chapter Four examines behavior in the workplace through a cost-benefit lens. Too often today, companies spend money in areas that don't support business objectives. This chapter offers a proposal to revisit the traditional productivity formula to include manageable human-capital costs in the denominator. Further, this chapter provides a recommendation to calculate manageable human-capital expenses, in a similar way that manufacturing would calculate the cost of waste. Specific research results are offered on the financial opportunity in increasing specific measures, such as organization, management, and growth-and-development ratings. Turnover costs and improvement savings are offered.

Chapter Five introduces EmployER Engagement through an action research model. Many organizations only attempt to get feedback from their employees once per year, through annual engagement surveys. This chapter shows why that is not enough. Companies need to consider ongoing self-study to direct and inform action requirements throughout the employee life cycle. For example, if organizations want to know how to improve productivity and retention of recent hires, new employees should be surveyed at multiple points throughout the onboarding process. To assess engagement opportunity and intent to stay, and to receive employee feedback on organizational policies, changes, and initiatives, periodic studies with incumbent employees should be utilized as an organizational reference for action requirements throughout the year. Finally, should employees choose to exit affiliation with the organization, employers must have accurate, comprehensive, and action-oriented data on why employees left and what the organization must do to improve engagement and retention. Most important, this chapter highlights the criticality of acting on valid data.

In total, these chapters provide you with the rationale and proven techniques to shift to an ROI and relationally balanced perspective, and the tactics necessary to become a preferred employer.

If You Take Anything Away from This Book, Take This

1. Successful organizations will find the people necessary to do the work that needs to get done.

2. Organizations know that employee engagement scores are not going up. Despite enormous increases in spending, employee engagement scores remain low. Doing more of the same is a mistake. As Gordo in the movie *Stand by Me* says, "Wagon Train is a really cool show, but did you ever notice that they never get anywhere? They just keep wagon training." Companies just keep surveying employee engagement, but they never get anywhere.

3. Attraction and retention are consequences of employee and employer engagement.

4. HR may have responsibility for recruitment, but Operations Management needs to be responsible and accountable for retention. Turnover expenses, direct and indirect, must be allocated to operational managers, their budgets, and their bonus opportunity. If an organization really wants to reduce turnover, start holding managers accountable.

5. Becoming a better employer requires ASKING, HEARING, COMMUNICATING, and ACTING.

6. Organizations can and must become Preferred and Engaged EmployERs.

ONE

THE CASE FOR EMPLOYER ENGAGEMENT – AN EXECUTIVE SUMMARY

Most earthquakes go unnoticed. Two sides of the earth push against each other, and yet their subtle shifts are recorded only by seismologists and maybe a few particularly attuned house pets. Minor tremors can be difficult to feel. But this time, it's different. The ground is finally shaking. It feels at times as if our entire world has started to crumble. Many of us never saw it coming.
—Claire Suddath (Bloomberg Businessweek, December 25, 2017)

We can't solve problems by using the same kind of thinking we used when we created them.
—Albert Einstein

Twenty years ago, I was invited to deliver the keynote address at a recruitment and retention conference in Las Vegas. In preparation for this event, I spoke with organizers to fully understand their objectives and then crafted the deliverables for my presentation entitled

"The Differing Preferences, Expectations, and Intents of an Emerging Workforce."

As it came time for the conference, I dined with conference leaders, further discussed the agenda, and confirmed our 8:45 a.m. sound check. At nine I sat in my chair and half listened to the association president deliver announcements and introduce me to five hundred attendees. As my anticipatory anxiety caught me thinking about how I would start the presentation, I concurrently reviewed the attendee handouts. The tab for my presentation was stamped EMPLOYEE ENGAGEMENT.

"And now, please join me in welcoming Dr. Mahan."

I walked up to the stage, shook hands with the conference leader, fumbled with the podium, and addressed the crowd. I usually began with humor or some mildly self-deprecating comment, but my feelings were conflicted, and I hardly knew how to start. Following what seemed to be too long a pause, I looked to the audience and requested that they take out their pens and open their manuals to the "Employee Engagement" tab in their conference binders.

I asked them to draw a heavy line, crossing out the last E in EMPLOYEE, and to insert an R at the end. I told them I was not going to talk about employee engagement . . . I was going to talk about EmployER Engagement.

EMPLOYER ENGAGEMENT

As organizational-behavior-management professionals, it is relatively common for business executives to tell us of the employee engagement strategies they have put in place. We hear their ideas about casual dress days, wine parties, cappuccino machines, new compensation plans, flexible schedules and work-from-home days, wellness apps, training, stock purchase plans, and bring-your-dog-to-work days. We hear about golf putting contests in the hallways, concierge services, and massage schedules. We also hear about their employee engagement surveys.

Then, being relatively decent listeners and a bit smart-alecky, we often inquire:

- Are employees staying longer?
- Are people lining up to come to work for you?
- Are manageable human-capital expenses going down?
- Are profits up?
- Is organizational productivity increasing?

Our questions prompt what appears to be thoughtfulness, but often these executives don't know or can't answer our inquiry. Sometimes they take on the countenance of Eeyore—the friendly but depressed donkey in Winnie the Pooh stories. They know their engagement scores are flat or failing. They are also just plain tired of it all, thinking and feeling helpless to resolve it. Sometimes they just wish they could outsource employees to a vendor, perhaps a staffing company, perhaps overseas.

Today, more than ever before, employee-centric needs assessment, aligned solutions, communications, and evaluation measures are critical to successfully executing a growth and productivity strategy. Today, it is necessary to understand the real reasons why people come to the organization, why people stay, and why people would or wouldn't work for the organization again in order to responsibly intervene, reduce human capital expense, and increase productivity.

Organizations continue to struggle with finding and keeping people and creating the workplace conditions necessary to drive productivity. Sometimes, in an effort to manage responsibly, companies are increasing budgets and resources, money and people, on engagement initiatives that simply do not work. Billions are spent on employee attraction, retention, and development, and yet employees remain disenchanted with their roles and disenfranchised from their companies. Companies are increasing recruitment personnel and expenses in an effort to bring people in to do the necessary work, but people are not staying. One in three American workers report they are chronically stressed on the job, and mainstream press reports that more than half of US workers are looking for new jobs.

Right or wrong, employee engagement seems to be the latest management panacea du jour. Some act as if it is the latest holy grail of management. However, dependence on ill-defined engagement is a serious mistake. Engagement is a promise to do something. Employee engagement connotes a promise by the employee—a pledge that they will do what they say they can do. This book is not arguing against employee engagement but alternatively arguing that companies and managers need to recognize engagement as a shared relationship wherein employers also own their promise to do what they say they will do.

Perhaps the reason results of employee engagement initiatives have been stagnant or diminishing is because they have been one-sided. The employee has owned the responsibility for engagement and has been punished for its absence. Companies have thrown money at popular (yet erroneous) engagement solutions that simply have not worked. One can only go so far to blame the employee for a company's faults before finally looking at the organization itself. A necessary tactic today is to ask and know what presenting organizational conditions enhance or compromise productivity and engagement.

Whether motivated by intentional benevolence or basic economic realities, today's employer can have a shared, collaborative employer-employee relationship. This chapter presents the advocacy position that companies need to fulfill their promise just as they expect employees to fulfill theirs. If the objective is to increase both employee and employer satisfaction and productivity, as in any relationship, it takes two. Two, employer and employee, is the win.

The economics are clear. The escalating competition for workers and a shrinking talent pool are coming together, intensifying an employee-in-control marketplace.[1] The need for trained, talented workers is growing faster than their availability as increasing job growth, decreasing unemployment, the shrinking number of available people, and increasing turnover all come together. With fewer qualified workers to fill growing jobs, employees have even more choice in where they will work, clearly giving the employee the power in the occupational marketplace.

With this power shift, companies must be more competitive in their recruitment, management, and retention strategies. Companies need to become preferred employers—employers who recognize that sustaining and growing their businesses requires skilled and available people. Companies that ignore employment trends relevant to their geography or industry will be compromised by not having the people to do the work that needs to be done. Attraction, recruiting, and retention costs will rise, significantly compromising growth and profitability. Employee turnover must and can be managed.

Is employee engagement the real solution? A sampling review of the thousands of professional and popular press articles on employee engagement offers differing perspectives across disciplines, with articles coming from managerial psychology, human resource management, organization development, industrial and organizational psychology, leadership, communications, management, economics, marketing, business, finance, and wellness. Some professional articles link engagement to business outcomes such as employee and customer satisfaction, productivity, employee retention, and profits.[2] Social media mostly offers feel-good guarantees on how to improve engagement. The popular press might provide links to websites where employee engagement is promised if you construct an online questionnaire. Some vendors will tout the wisdom of their twelve-, twenty-four-, or one-hundred-question survey and its ability to measure engagement in an organization. Engagement instrument design might direct one to anything from a three- to a twelve- to a sixteen-point rating scale. Much of what we are told is contradictory and confusing.

While the literature presents passionate arguments both for and against employee engagement, scientific support for either side is lacking.[3] Dozens of studies and meta-analyses report the limitations of employee engagement meaning, measurement, and business results.[4] Despite serious concerns about the validity of defining and measuring employee engagement, companies continue to seek commercially available, one-size-fits-all engagement surveys. One need only do an online search for "employee engagement surveys" to see the massive scope of this multibillion-dollar—and still growing—survey industry.

Definitions of employee engagement range from an important business-outcome breakthrough to the most popular manage-by-best-seller buzzword.[5] Many contemporary and popular definitions come from consulting companies with ready solutions. It is quite interesting to see how often various vendors' employee-engagement-survey results align so well with prepackaged solution offerings in the same vendors' product lines. Coincidence? We think not.

If you ask ten "expert" consultants to define engagement, you will probably get ten different responses. If you ask how they will determine the engagement of your employee population, this is when it really gets slippery. Often well-intentioned companies are unknowingly paying vendors for biased surveys where results dictate the same vendor's products and services. For instance, the study conducted by a benefits company recommends the redesign of benefits; the one offered by a recruitment software company requires the adoption of their ERP technology; a leadership development firm, of course, proposes their leadership development and coaching curriculum; and a generational expert likely tells you that you need to start profiling employees based on their age. A recent advertisement in a sponsored human-resource newsletter reported the results of a study specifying that engagement is increased with lunch breaks. You guessed it: the study and the ad were placed by a cafeteria supply company. And the list goes on.

There is no real science to back up a methodology for identifying or measuring employee engagement. Some experts would even call engagement a myth. Regardless, without a clear and common definition, the understanding and implementation of solutions for employee engagement remain cluttered, scattered, and unfocused.

There are six things we know to be true:

1. Employees can know what they expect from an employer.
2. Employees can know how they want to be treated by their supervisors.
3. Employees can know how to create a better workplace.
4. As employers create better workplaces, employees will stay longer, be more productive and innovative, and create better relationships with coworkers and customers.
5. Employee attitude and satisfaction drive increased retention, and increased retention reduces human capital costs.
6. Employee attitude and satisfaction drive customer attitude and satisfaction, and customer satisfaction drives growth, and profitability.

The key to increasing employee attitude and satisfaction, perhaps creating an engaged workforce, is easy: ASK, HEAR, COMMUNI-CATE, and ACT.

Sure, on the surface employee engagement sounds good. The very mention of "employee engagement" has face validity, and it resonates with business and HR leaders. The term itself is ubiquitous. Vendors' sales language broadcasts that they increase employee engagement. Popular literature implies that the journey to increasing growth and profit solely rests in harnessing employee engagement. Many companies are led (erroneously) to believe there is a causal relationship between engagement and profitability.

Companies are buying it, but many of them are just wasting money. Many companies have fallen victim to the popularity of the term, the remedy promised by employee engagement. It's increasingly difficult to find a company recruitment communication that doesn't address their employee engagement proposition.

Companies spend money on surveys and occasionally use results to determine change objectives. Some even act on defined objectives. These actions sometimes present additional financial risk to companies that implement programs based on the results of compromised studies. Yet companies keep buying services from vendors promising to improve engagement. Employer, be cautious.

The absence of valid measurement tools seriously calls into question the validity of results, recommendations, and subsequent action.

The objectives for employee engagement appear to differ throughout organizations. While the HR objective may be to increase attraction and retention, the business objective is to increase operational efficiencies (reduce the ratio of human capital expenses to operating expenses); increase competitive position, including keeping the best-of-the-best workforce; and increase growth and profit.

Employee engagement practices largely have not succeeded with these objectives. The promises of the consultants to reduce manageable costs and increase engagement are not being met. Expenses related to recruiting, hiring, training, behavior risk, and turnover are increasing, and employee engagement is either stagnant or on the decline.[6] Many of the best people are choosing to quit, and yet companies continue to throw good money after bad. In 2016, the learning and talent development market, including engagement, was valued at $32.4 billion. It is expected to grow to $53.4 billion by 2020.[7] While this may be good for learning and talent development providers, it may be of questionable value to companies.

Employee engagement was initially conceptualized by William Kahn, PhD, then professor of organizational behavior at Boston University's Questrom School of Business. Personnel engagement was partially defined as "the harnessing of organization members' selves to their work roles."[8] Other adopted definitions define engagement as a state of mind characterized by vigor, dedication, and absorption;[9] vigor across physical, emotional and cognitive dimensions—specifically, feelings of physical strength, emotional energy, and cognitive liveliness;[10] and a function of personality.[11] The consensus is that engagement is a state of mind characterized by activation in what the individual is doing.[12]

Harnessing is both an interesting and a concerning word as applied in today's workplace. While one can be reasonably confident that it was not Dr. Kahn's intent to suggest employees be yoked for performance, many companies continue to act as if this is the case. Perhaps this is legacy behavior representative of a time when there were more people than there were jobs, or a time when employees were dependent on a company and had few options other than one employer. It might just be part of traditional managers' denial that things are changing. Regardless, the days of the employee being dependent on the employer are easing, disappearing, or gone. To succeed, companies must change their perspective. Employees are not yoked, or harnessed, to a company.

Companies must shift away from their employer view of the work relationship and instead start looking through the employee lens.

This is the challenge offered in the preface. A person looking through a manager's lens is likely to view situations differently than a person looking through an employee lens. Where the manager may be pressured by the volume of work that needs to be accomplished, the employee may be troubled by not knowing exactly how to do the necessary work. The manager, in time, may get angry due to the lack of task completion and define it as a performance (behavior) issue, while the employee defines it as a training (skill) issue. They could both be troubled by the volume of work that needs to be accomplished, but for different reasons. And that is part of the problem. They may be saying the same thing but meaning different things. The interventions differ. Looking through the traditional employer lens in an employee-in-control economy is the mistake.

The way you label a situation dictates the way you respond to the situation. Correct data informs. Absent, incomplete, or inaccurate data does not inform, or it misinforms.

Errors in employee engagement definitions and measurement, denial of current economic conditions, and traditional ways of viewing the employee perspective each contribute to today's attraction, retention, and engagement crisis. Despite promises, many conventional employee-engagement initiatives are (1) in conflict with the current economy; (2) methodologically flawed; and/or (3) compromised by well-intentioned but misinformed ethics and value practices.

IN CONFLICT WITH THE CURRENT ECONOMY

Trends in the United States illustrate a thriving economy in which the number of available jobs and the competition for workers are each sharply increasing. Over the past nine years, job growth has been on the rise and unemployment has been on the decline. The changes since 2010 are significant: the unemployment rate has been cut in half, and job openings have increased over 70 percent, to more than seven million open jobs.

Along with job growth and lower unemployment, more workers are choosing to leave their jobs. Total separations have gone up 36 percent since 2010, largely driven by an 80 percent increase in voluntary quits. Jobs are opening faster than employers can fill them, and workers are increasingly selective about where and how they choose to work.

The talent pool is shrinking, and the demand for workers is exceeding current supply. The marketplace shifted from nearly seven unemployed persons to every one job opening in 2009 to a historic low of 1:1 unemployed-persons-to-job ratio in 2017 (1:1/2 in health care).[13] As of March 2018, there were more job openings than unemployed workers. Put simply: the number of jobs continues to increase, while the number of job seekers continues to decrease. Openings are outpacing hiring. As the 2019 US plans for infrastructure funding and development move forward and restrictions on immigration continue, this will reach levels well surpassing the talent war of the late 1990s and early 2000s. In forward-looking projections, the Bureau of Labor Statistics expects even further job growth and a talent pool that cannot keep pace. A large portion of the population is reaching retirement age, while not enough workers are obtaining the skills required to fill growing occupations.

Employee poaching is and will remain a standard recruitment practice.

Trends around job growth apply to some occupations and industries more than others. Almost 95 percent of the job growth between 2014 and 2024 is expected to come from service-related sectors, 41 percent of which will come from health care and social assistance industries. One also needs to pay attention to trends around the types of workers required to fill these roles. Health care and technical occupations will realize the largest growth and together account for about a quarter of all new jobs by 2024. Within this growth, of the fifteen occupations expected to grow the fastest, eleven of them will require training beyond what is currently required for a high school diploma.

Turnover encompasses employees who are leaving their jobs, whether it be a voluntary decision made by the employee or an involuntary decision made by the company. Regardless of the type of turnover, when an employee leaves the company incurs direct costs through actual financial expenses and indirect costs through decreased organizational performance, lost institutional knowledge, and employee and customer brand-reputation compromises.

Aside from attraction and recruitment costs, demand exceeding supply, and stagnant engagement, the cost of employee turnover to companies is high, even by conservative estimates. These costs are taking a toll on company profits and organizational performance. While there is not an agreed-upon standard for determining the cost of turnover, some studies have calculated the direct cost of turnover by adding up costs across separation, replacement, and training activities, while others consider percentages or multiples of the employee's salary. Estimates have ranged from $4,000 or more per employee, to one-third of annualized compensation, to one and a half to two times the employee's annual salary or more.

Given a median wage for US workers in 2018 of $44,546 per year, the one-third cost is approximately $15,000 per separation. Even the lowest estimate amounts to significant direct costs for an organization. Indirect costs of turnover are sometimes referred to as "productivity costs" and come from lost institutional knowledge, the time lag it takes to find a replacement, and the time it takes for that new worker to become fully productive.[14]

Following the turnover estimate of $15,000 per employee, in 2018 the Bureau of Labor Statistics reported 40,081,000 voluntary separations (quits), amounting to $601 billion in costs to employers. This reflects a 12 percent increase from 2016, where 35,839,000 voluntary separations cost $538 billion. If the voluntary quit rate continues as projected, voluntary turnover costs alone will increase to nearly $679 billion in 2020, a 19 percent increase from 2017. Employee engagement initiatives are not accomplishing desired results.

Based on approximately 250,000 employee interviews conducted by the Work Institute, 77 percent of the most important reasons employees quit are preventable by employers.[15] Generalizing 77 percent to the forty million employees who voluntarily quit suggests that thirty-one million resignations were preventable if employers had chosen to intervene in the correct areas. Should employers make the correct decisions and select aligned interventions, a mere 10 percent reduction would result in 3.1 million employees retained, roughly the population of Chicago.

METHODOLOGICALLY FLAWED

In the absence of data, a person is uninformed. With bad data, a person is misinformed. Methodological errors in employee engagement result from definitional concerns, questionnaire/survey development, administration, data analysis, reporting, communication, and action. Many of today's employee engagement methods are neither reliable nor valid. The reasons include:

- inaccurate collection, analysis, interpretation, presentation, or organization of data, including invalid comparisons between similar-appearing data;

- measures that may not be surveying employee engagement but instead ratings of job control/autonomy, coworker support, supervision, coaching, feedback, training, task significance, problem-solving, compensation, rewards, or recognition;

- misinterpretation of ratings scales;

- errors in scoring;

- mistaking correlation for causation—thinking because something follows, it was caused by something preceding (the *post hoc, ergo propter hoc* fallacy);

- analysis paralysis—thinking survey administration, data gathering, and analysis and obsessive reanalysis of results is a worthy exercise;

- assuming enterprise-wide results are representative of group, individual, geographic, or role-specific requirements;

- failing to communicate accurate results;

- failing to act on accurate results; and

- implementing solutions that are driven by false results, often by predetermined solutions bias.

Companies are unique in their location-specific climate, history, and workplace conditions, as well as in the preferences, expectations, and intents of workers.

Typical and popular models for measuring employee engagement and retention impose specific lists of workplace conditions that employees must rate. Employees typically are given a list of items and asked to rate the items on a scale. However, and to the detriment of accuracy, items usually are drawn from subject areas that the employer has historically thought important, rather than items identified as important by employees. For example, an employee is typically asked to rate satisfaction with pay, benefits, supervisors, company mission, recognition, colleagues, growth opportunity, supervisory behavior, and how likely the respondent is to recommend employment to a friend or colleague. While these are not bad questions, they are self-limiting in that they only allow the employee to respond to predetermined and often biased themes. How many times have you filled out a survey tool that either didn't allow you to identify your real concern or limited your evaluation to an individual rather than the company he or she represents? This is an employer-in-control model. And in today's environment, it simply does not work.

Looking at reasons for leaving among those who exit tells only half the story. It is critical to interview current employees to understand the real reasons they stay with a company, to both predict intent to stay and accurately build a retention and engagement strategy.

Alternatively, and responsive to an employee-in-control market, open-ended questions around simple and known core drivers of attitudes and subsequent behaviors provide deeper probing into the "why," bringing to light the most important workplace issues from the employee perspective. For example, having employees identify concerns most important to them, to rate those most important concerns, and to identify what would need to happen to increase that rating specifically identifies necessary action requirements.

Why do you plan on staying for a long time?

What else, what else, what else?

Of these reasons, which is the most important?

Approaching employee impressions with an open-ended method allows the employee to voice his or her real workplace observations and concerns, without limiting the responses. Identifying the most important workplace strengths (drivers) and weaknesses (restraints) illuminates areas necessary for improvement.

COMPROMISED (PERHAPS) BY WELL-INTENTIONED BUT MISINFORMED ETHICS AND VALUE PRACTICES

In its 2000 annual report, Enron touted communication, respect, and integrity as core values. *Fortune* magazine named Enron "America's Most Innovative Company" for six consecutive years.[16] Enron's audit firm, Arthur Andersen, listed its core values as trust and accountability.[17] Arthur Andersen surrendered its licenses to practice after being found guilty of criminal charges, resulting in job loss for 85,000 employees.

Many organizations prioritize attention to defining, posting, marketing, and branding their ethics and values. Company websites list them as part of an employment offer to potential candidates, post them throughout work locations, and tout them in annual reports. Some companies are diligent in making sure values are evidenced in daily behaviors. However, in many organizations, especially those that operate with traditional roles, practices, policies, and procedures, ethics and company values postings are often empty words—or noise. These are the companies where employees are expected to respect the pressures and objectives of managers, yet managers make little effort to understand and acknowledge employee concerns. These companies may identify respect as a value, but willfully or unknowingly dismiss, invalidate, or marginalize employees.

Ageism, school-ism, GPA-ism, degree-ism, gender-ism, regional-ism, and other (not illegal) unfounded and unreasonable discriminations spread, mostly unchecked, in today's workplace. As subtle as the previously mentioned biases, many companies also tolerate "employee-ism," perhaps defined as a belief that one's own grade level makes one superior and that lower-grade-level employees are inferior.

> A few years ago I was working with a Fortune 50 company, assisting with the human side of an acquisition. Needing some work space, I was directed to a fantastic office, high in the sky with windows overlooking a major city. I could literally see into three states. It was a splendid work space, but it was loud. You see, maintenance staff were present, moving walls and rearranging offices. As I took a break to refill my coffee, I had the opportunity to speak with these maintenance professionals. They were tearing up bordered carpeting and covering windows with cubicle partitions. This was being done in preparation for new employees who were to be stationed in this renovated area. You see, they told me, the employees who were moving into this space were not of sufficient grade level to warrant either bordered carpet or windows.
>
> —Thomas F. Mahan

AT-RISK EMPLOYERS

Assuming job openings exceed employee availability, companies at risk are those who refuse to acknowledge the importance of the employee experience. These are the companies whose management is not listening to the employees. These are the managers living in denial, somehow believing that employees are handcuffed/harnessed/yoked and will continue to tolerate being ignored or compromised, when employees have a clear path to go elsewhere. These are the companies that foster an "us versus them" mentality, where managers (who are also employees) convey that only certain grade levels can have ideas or only certain groups are worthy of change, promotion, windows, bordered carpet, travel, or parking spaces. Perhaps the implication heard is that the company is only for the certain credentialed few, and that others need to "know their place." There was a time, in a damaged economy, when managers were free to say, "If you don't like it here, leave." In today's economy, managers can no longer afford to lose employees, as quit rates and quit costs are at an all-time high.

A management philosophy that believes employees are unimportant or management practices that (intentionally or unintentionally) invalidate employee thoughts and feelings marginalize a company's workforce. Examples of employee engagement marginalization in today's work environments include

- emphasizing engagement as an employee responsibility instead of an organization responsibility;
- implying lower engagement is attributable to employee inadequacies;
- presuming that employees, in their subordinate roles, have control over their organization's climate;
- negating or dismissing employee experiences, preferences, or

expectations;

- employing compromised methodologies, yet believing one is measuring what needs to be measured;

- failing to provide feedback to employees, including communications regarding subsequent actions to be taken as a result of an employee survey;

- stereotyping employees based on age, gender, geography, or role; and

- promoting based on time-in-grade rather than achievement.

EMPLOYEES DON'T NEED YOU— YOU NEED THEM

It's a new time. Today, when the employee is needed by the employer more than the employer is needed by the employee, organizations either thrive or perish. Those that perish may be the organizations run by managers in denial of the fact that change is a requirement, much like the publishing executives of the '90s who denied what was previously made known in the crash of music publishing. These are the cable entertainment companies and the banks that honor themselves as employee- and customer-centric, yet ignore the recommendations, feelings, and thoughts of an increasingly stressed-out, understaffed, and high-turnover employee population. These are the organizations with electronic phone banks, expecting employees and consumers to press too many buttons to reach someone who will instruct them to call yet another number. "Please listen carefully as all our codes have changed." No. They haven't.

These are the phone companies that don't have a phone number, or the hospital corporations who centralize scheduling and expect medical office staff and doctors to bear the brunt of dissatisfied employees who call for schedules and patients who call for appointments or prescription refills. These are the companies whose "efficiencies" serve to create punishing conditions, causing nurses and technicians to seek new employers.

Do managers who made decisions to implement call trees in their companies see the complaints (and stress) handled by the employees who (eventually) answer the phone? Implementing so-called efficiencies that create negative employee and customer experiences is disrespectful to employees and customers alike. Furthermore, these practices marginalize employees and customers.

Employers would do well to look at the relationship between the working conditions created through understaffing and their employee and customer turnover. In the past few weeks, one of this book's authors requested assistance from an automotive service department, a cable TV/Internet company, a retained computer service provider, a bank, and a physician's office (all, by the way, high-turnover industries). In every case, while the employee did his or her best to provide assistance, the staffing, training, organization procedural expectations, or technology restricted the employee's ability to be helpful.

In several of the aforementioned experiences, a survey followed the call. Of alarm, the survey did not provide a way to express dissatisfaction without negatively evaluating the individual who tried to help. The problem is often not the employee but instead the organizational conditions employers expect employees and customers to work within. How is one able to complete a survey when the questions are artificial or restrict content? While I don't blame the employee, I will seriously consider dismissing the retained computer service, changing my bank, and switching Internet and cable provider.

Companies that thrive in the next several years will be those that acknowledge the requirement to create the necessary organizational conditions that attract and retain employees and customers while re-attracting, thus retaining, the employees and customers they already have. The managers in these companies will listen to employees and do everything they can, constantly and creatively pivoting to ever-evolving employee preferences, expectations, and intents.

Today's journey requires EmployER Engagement and a climate wherein the employer listens, understands, communicates, and responds to the employee perspective, just in time.

"You know the greatest danger facing us is ourselves, an irrational fear of the unknown. But there's no such thing as the unknown— only things temporarily hidden, temporarily not understood."
—Captain James T. Kirk

TWO

THE LANDSCAPE

There are plenty of people to do all the work you need doing.
They are just working somewhere else.

Founded by veteran health professionals, Renal Advantage Inc. (RAI), which was purchased by Fresenius in 2016, was one of the nation's leading providers of dialysis services. RAI was formed when two dialysis service providers, DaVita Inc. and Gambro Healthcare, merged. After the merger, with over 135 freestanding centers nationwide and additional centers developing rapidly, RAI leadership was interested to see exactly how their employees were affected. RAI faced a predicted 20 percent gap in the supply and demand of nurses by 2020 as well as the knowledge that 17 percent of health-care workers were dissatisfied. They needed to figure out how to retain their employees and avoid high turnover. RAI wasn't alone in this dilemma. Many companies face high turnover and compromised employee retention.

The history of growth and profitability is the history of people at work. We hunted and farmed; then we hunted and farmed for others. The hunter killed more game, and the farmer grew more corn. As sales and bartering opportunities to receptive consumers grew, the hunter hired helpers to get more pelts and the farmer secured more land, hired more hands, plowed more fields, and sold more corn.

As a continued growth and profitability strategy, the hunters and ranchers raised pigs, chickens, and cattle; invested in more land; and built fences. They planted seed, then planted more seed. Increased product required increased hands to harvest. The Mr. Peabodys put people into the mines with pick and shovel and then figured out how to take more out of the mines, quicker. We built horse-drawn wagons to transport crop and product and hired more people to haul goods. We laid track across the continent, a competition dependent on Asian and European immigrants racing to the Utah Territory. We built companies to make fences and then hired more people to make more fences. Knowing we could do it better, quicker, and cheaper, Mr. Ford put us on assembly lines and then built more assembly lines. Horse whips and incandescent lamps became a thing of the past, and people found new places where they could put bread on their tables in exchange for labor. Sometimes they relocated, moving to find work. Electricity created more jobs, garbage collection created even more jobs, and a pharmaceutical industry was formed from aspirin in the late 1800s.

The economic crash of 1929 forced mass unemployment, and on March 21, 1933, President Roosevelt proposed to Congress the establishment of the Civilian Conservation Corps (CCC). Ten days later it was approved by the Seventy-Third Congress. By April 5, a director was in place, and five days later, on April 10, 1933, twenty-five thousand workers were enrolled. Within months, at least 450,000 CCC families had received paychecks.

Wars continued, and the military industrial complex hired larger percentages of the workforce. Because people will always need to eat and will always require doctors, food and health-care industries formed and grew.

Growth and profitability through leveraging tangible assets worked well in the agricultural economy. As weather conditions permitted, farmers, ranchers, and corporations successfully leveraged wheat, corn, and cattle with fertile land and consumers. Likewise, growth and profitability worked in the manufacturing economy. World War II, trade agreements, and the destruction of manufacturing in England, Germany, and Japan built the American manufacturing empire. Manufacturing plants, raw materials, real estate, equipment, and inventory created consumer-ready products and government-ready infrastructure. In time, as a labor-cost-savings tactic, manufacturers left US borders, while service and technology industries became the fuel that fed the GDP.

How we choose to work and live, how we choose to relate to one other, and how we meet our safety and security requirements change regularly in response to market conditions. Off-shoring, Internet speed, consumer preferences, trade policies, cyber security, cloud computing, the elimination of and the rebuilding of borders, and threats of terrorism have effected a major shift in the US economy. Agricultural and manufacturing economies were dependent on leveraging hard assets, and while some would argue that today's economy is defined by technology, it is based instead on leveraging human behavior. In today's service economy, companies are increasingly dependent on people, and companies need to be prepared to access and leverage skilled, able, and willing employees.

At present, employees can make a choice of where and how they want to work and who they want to work with more readily and easily than ever before. There was a time when people were tethered to a company because of health care, pensions, geography, or limited job availability. Medical insurance portability, the elimination of preexisting-condition barriers, 401(k) products, and transportation largely relaxed those ties. The new realities surrounding improved job availability leave employees unfettered and harness-free. Workers are more mobile than ever and can choose to exploit that mobility.

Today's leaders who expect to execute their growth and profitability plans must acknowledge employee choices and create the organizational conditions necessary to attract and retain the people required to do the work that needs to be done.

Several marketplace realities are worth exploring:

- The US economy is flowing steadily.

- Workforce supply is at a trickle.

- Job openings continue to rise.

- Worker shortage is increasing.

- Voluntary quits are at historic highs.

- First-year employees are at highest risk.

- We can know why employees are leaving.

THE US ECONOMY IS FLOWING STEADILY

The US has seen recessions since the 1930s' Depression, but nothing compared to what occurred from 2008 until mid-2009. Some call it the Great Recession, and many have opinions on why and how it happened. Regardless of the blame and honorific debates, the US economy and its people demonstrated resilience. Since 2009, the look and feel of a booming economy remain on the rise.

The gross domestic product (GDP) in the US has grown consistently since 2012, and for now, the outlook for continued growth appears positive. Housing has rebounded, banks have stabilized, infrastructure plans are being considered, and manufacturing is beginning to make a comeback.

Jobs are a worthy result of economic growth. As of April 2019, the unemployment level was at 3.6 percent (the lowest level since the 1960s), and job openings continued to rise. In 2018 alone, over 2.5 million jobs were added to the US economy. Job growth is expected to continue for some time.

WORKFORCE SUPPLY IS AT A TRICKLE

The laws of supply and demand typically apply in the buying, selling, and pricing of goods and services. When excess houses are on the market, prices stabilize or decline, additional incentives are offered, and we have what is referred to as a buyers' market. A sellers' market occurs when limited houses are available in a growing geographic market. Prices increase, regardless of whether the kitchen, bathroom, and landscaping are upgraded.

So too, economic laws of supply and demand apply to work and the workforce. An employer-in-control market occurs when the supply of workers exceeds the number of jobs available. In this environment, there are plenty of people to do the work that needs to be done, and companies typically have control of the employment relationship, including how they choose to treat and compensate employees. When job availability exceeds the supply of workers, the market becomes one of employee-in-control. In this environment, employees have the choice to define and comanage the employment relationship.

Supply/Demand (in thousands)

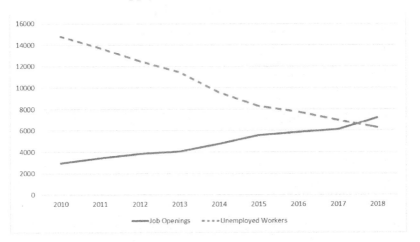

The supply of employees participating in the workforce is declining and will continue to decline over the next several years. The US is likely to experience an employee-in-control market for the near future for several reasons, chiefly the following:

- Since the early 1990s, the US population growth has been trending down while job growth has been trending up.

- Current workers are moving into age groups with lower participation rates. Today, the median age of the labor force is forty-two years. By 2026, this is expected to be 43.2 years. As the labor force continues to get older, the overall labor force participation rate is projected to decrease to 61 percent in 2026. This rate is down from 62.8 percent in 2016 and from the peak of 67.1 percent in 2000, prior to the 2007–09 recession.

- Future/potential workers are decreasing their participation rate. Participation of younger workers, ages sixteen to twenty-four, is on the decline as more people in this age group seek post-secondary degrees.

- The US is not currently recognized as a preferred place for foreign workers to relocate. Immigration policy, and its ensuant sentiment, is a limiting factor on foreign-born persons' choices to work or study in the US. While this is managed largely as a political issue, the marketplace and the requirements for workers may ultimately drive and revise immigration policy.

Labor Force Participation Rate

Year	Age Group 16–24	25–54	55 & Older
1996	65.5	83.8	30.3
2006	60.6	82.9	38
2016	55.2	81.3	40
2026	52.5	81.6	38.9

JOB OPENINGS CONTINUE TO RISE

The US Bureau of Labor Statistics (BLS) has consistently reported over seven million open jobs since April 2018, at a time when unemployment levels were below what economists traditionally consider full employment. During the Great Recession, unemployment levels reached historic highs. Almost 10 percent of all US workers were unemployed. As the economy began its rebound in 2009, the unemployment rate began to decline rapidly as companies once again expanded and hired from the ranks of the unemployed.

Economists explain a certain level of unemployment as the natural unemployment rate. The natural unemployment rate is largely made up of employees who are in some type of job or career transition; generally it is not made up of the long-term unemployed. In April 2019, unemployment rates reached a low 3.6 percent. As the natural unemployment rate is measured at 4.5–5 percent, the actual unemployment rate remains even lower. The Congressional Budget Office projects this trend to continue through 2027.

As the unemployment rate has fallen and the economy continues to add jobs, more and more job openings are going unfilled. Since 2009, the annual average number of open jobs waiting to be filled in the US has increased by over 155 percent. February 2019 was the 101st consecutive month of job growth. The US economy added twenty million jobs from 2010 to 2019. In November 2018, the US hit a record number of unfilled job openings of over 7.6 million, indicating that labor demand is at an all-time high. Job openings are projected to increase as the economy continues to grow over the next decade. Employers will continue to struggle to find workers to fill open positions.

WORKER SHORTAGE IS INCREASING

In 2008, the beginnings of the most recent recession, the number of unemployed people per job opening was 1.9, rising to a high point of 6.6 in July 2009. It has trended steadily down since then, ranging from 1.3 to 1.4 in each month in 2016. Now, it's about 1:1 (0.5 to 1 in health care), which is comparable to the levels in the early 2000s, during the so-called "war for talent." Put simply: the number of jobs continues to increase, while the number of job seekers continues to decrease.[18]

The demand for workers is increasing significantly, and job growth is exceeding the number of available workers. According to Bureau of Labor Statistics Employment Projections 2016–2026, employment is projected to increase by 11.5 million.[19] This represents an increase from 156.1 million to 167.6 million. Health-care industries and their associated occupations are expected to account for a larger share of new jobs as aging populations drive health-care-service demand.

From 2016 to 2026, overall occupational employment is anticipated to grow by 7.4 percent, which is an increase from 2014–2024 projections.[20] Production and farming occupations are the only occupational groups forecast to experience a decline during this period.

VOLUNTARY QUITS ARE AT HISTORIC HIGHS

Back in 2000, the real-life story of The Perfect Storm was brought to life by George Clooney, Mark Wahlberg, and Diane Lane. The story tracked the plight of commercial fishermen working in the lucrative yet dangerous occupation of fishing the North Atlantic. Just off the northeastern seaboard, three storm systems combined to create a massive weather event that engulfed the fishing boat Andrea Gail. She never returned to port. Current workforce conditions are creating a similar storm triumvirate. Job openings, unemployment, and the quit rate are all trending in the direction that does not favor an employer's objective for productivity or growth.

—Danny A. Nelms

Current workforce conditions are creating a similar storm triumvirate. Job openings, unemployment, and the quit rate are all trending in the direction that does not favor an employer's objective for productivity or growth.

With fewer available workers, supply-and-demand economics is redefining employee options. Given current conditions, workers have choice opportunities. One of those choices is the option to quit, and workers are voluntarily leaving their jobs at historic levels.

Total separations are comprised of voluntary (employee-initiated) and involuntary (employer-directed) separations. While overall total separations have not increased in any meaningful way since 2009, employer-directed layoffs and discharges declined in 2010 and again in 2013, leveled off, and appear to be trending down again. Voluntary separations, on the other hand, rose for the ninth consecutive year in 2018, representing an increase in the willingness and ability of employees to leave a job.

Total separations are being driven by employees, not employers.

In 2017, BLS reported 35.8 million employees quit their jobs in the US. This is an increase of over two million employees from the previous year.[21] Since 2009, the average annual number of employees who voluntarily leave (excluding retirement and relocation) has increased by over 80 percent, surpassing prerecession levels.

The relationship between organizational performance and turnover is statistically significant and negative. More than one in four employees (28.6 percent) voluntarily quit their jobs some time in 2018. That represents a total of over forty million employees who voluntarily exited their jobs (up from 35.8 million in 2017).

Turnover compromises organizational performance. Voluntary turnover hurts organizations more than involuntary turnover.

Employee turnover is a symptom of employers' not doing enough to select the right employees and create the conditions wherein employees stay and are most productive. Poor conditions are evidenced by absenteeism, presentee-ism, waste, safety concerns, complaints, worker's compensation claims, poor productivity, inappropriate behavior, and compliance violations.

Clearly, the best indicator of poor employment conditions is voluntary turnover. Many organizations are at a tipping point because employees are at a tipping point with alternate and available job options. When conditions in the job marketplace are favorable, and employers are not meeting employee preferences and expectations in their current roles, employees can and will leave.

FIRST-YEAR EMPLOYEES ARE AT HIGHEST RISK

When looking at turnover and turnover costs, it is important to consider the length of time an employee has been with a company. Employees who leave within their first year could cost companies more than employees who have been with a company longer before leaving. It may take employees three to six months on the job before they have added enough value to offset the cost of their recruitment, selection, hiring, orientation, onboarding, and compensation and benefits. When employees leave within their first year of employment, employers may never realize a return on the hiring investment.

In 2018, 38.6 percent of all turnover was attributed to employees who quit their jobs in their first year of employment, up from 34 percent in 2016. This follows an eight-year trend, with first-year turnover increasing since 2010.

% of Quitting Employees that Do So Within 365 Days

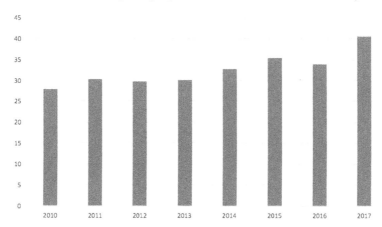

Employees who leave in their first year leave quickly. About half of employees who leave during year one do so within the first ninety days. If an employee makes it past the ninety-day mark, there's still a 20 percent chance he or she will quit before the end of the year

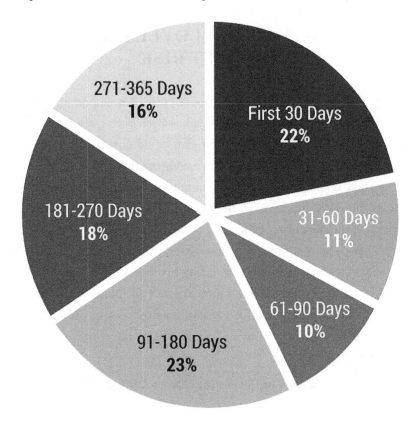

![megaphone icon] **STOP AND THINK**

Thirty-eight percent of all turnover is attributed to employees who quit in their first year. What are the consequences of 38 percent of your product or service failing in the first year?

What percentage of your employees quit in the first year?

Of the more controllable reasons for leaving in 2018, those who quit within the first year cited work-life balance, career development, manager behavior, job characteristics, and work environment as the most important reasons for leaving.

But what about your organization? Why are employees quitting in the first year?

What are you doing to solve this?
(Hint: the solution is not to hire more recruiters.)

WE CAN KNOW WHY EMPLOYEES ARE DISENGAGED AND LEAVING

Disengagement and turnover are huge costs to organizations, and problems many attempt, yet fail, to solve. Researchers and academics have published countless studies and theories on the causes of turnover, showing that job satisfaction, organizational commitment, and job-searching behaviors are most predictive of intent to leave.[22]

Given today's economic conditions and occupational options, exploring why employees choose to stay or leave, and thoroughly understanding and acting on real employee stay preferences and expectations, is fundamental. In the absence of desired workplace conditions, employees will quit their jobs.

Over the past twenty years, the Work Institute has developed a methodology to ask, listen, and capture the most important reasons employees leave their jobs. Based on insights from over 250,000 employees from various industries, workplace researchers conducted interviews and categorized results. These results were then coded into distinct reasons for leaving, representing ten categories,[23] accounting for 98.5 percent of the reasons employees leave or intend to leave. In 2018, reasons and frequency included the following:

- Career development: lack of opportunities for growth, achievement, and security (22.2 percent)
- Work-life balance: travel and scheduling preferences (12 percent)
- Manager behavior: absence of positive and productive relationships (11.3 percent)
- Compensation and benefits: total rewards promised vs. received (9.6 percent)
- Well-being: physical, emotional, and family-related issues (8.4 percent)
- Job characteristics: lack of ownership and enjoyment in manageable work (8.1 percent)
- Work environment: physical and cultural surroundings (5.2 percent)

- Relocation (10.2 percent)

- Involuntary (6.7 percent)

- Retirement (6.3 percent)

A review of these top ten categories for leaving in 2018 shows that 76 percent of turnover was more preventable as compared to 23.2 percent that was less preventable.

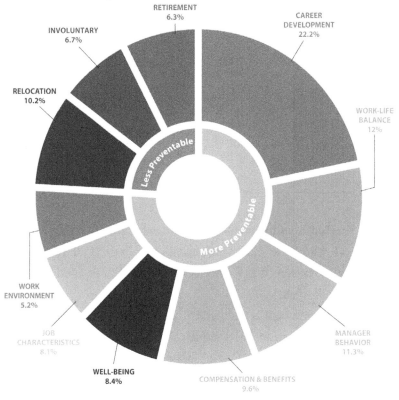

![icon] **STOP AND THINK**

Is it the employee or the employer who is disengaged? Is it both?

Where do you need to intervene?

With the employee?

With the employer?

With the workplace conditions?

Career development includes opportunities for growth, achievement, and security. Career development reasons have been on the rise more than any other reason. It is a priority for the workforce and key to a decision to quit a job.

Career development accounted for 22.2 percent of all reasons employees left their jobs in 2018, which marked the ninth consecutive year that the career development category led reasons for turnover. This rise occurred as the economy expanded, businesses flourished, and the fear of layoffs and staff reductions gave way to the desire to grow and advance one's career in an attractive job, or a preferred occupational role.

"Type of work" led the career development category at 33.1 percent, indicating that if employees didn't like the work they were doing, they could easily make a career change or find a more attractive job. Type of work surged as a reason for leaving from 2010 to 2014 as the economy recovered and opportunities increased. It's important to understand that when an employee leaves due to type of work, this doesn't mean he or she left for a promotion. It could indicate a lateral move or a shift to a completely different role.

Trends of reasons within the career development category reveal a desire to grow. Lack of growth and development as a reason for leaving rose to 24.6 percent in 2018, an increase of 170 percent since 2010. When growth and development opportunities were cited, employees mentioned a general chance to grow, acquire new skills, or better use the skills they have.

As the economy continued to rebound, employees who sought a promotion likely realized those opportunities, as reasons attributed to promotion and advancement declined to 14 percent in 2018, reflecting a 45.8 percent decrease since 2010. When promotion or advancement was cited as a reason, employees mentioned a perception that they could not move up, or a feeling that they were in a dead-end job.

The decision to return to school accounted for 18.4 percent, nearly one-fifth of the reasons for leaving within the career development category. This measure should be watched carefully. While it may appear that more young people are seeking higher education, this could reflect legacy recession behavior when students sought advanced degrees rather than being unemployed, as jobs were simply not available. A related measure that requires watching is the college degree requirement. Limited observation suggests that the historical requirement is shifting from "degree required" to "degree preferred" to the elimination of degree necessity. Ernst and Young (EY) recently decided that while academic qualifications remain an important consideration, they are not a barrier to getting employed. EY has found no evidence to correlate success in higher education with professional success.[24]

As career opportunities increase elsewhere, employers must take steps to understand the needs, preferences, and goals of their workers, or miss out on opportunities to keep talent that they need.

It is important to note that, although career development remains the largest theme, there are differences across companies. For example, 14 percent of organizations do not have career development in their employees' top three reasons for leaving.

Employers ask, "What if we develop our employees and they leave us?" What they should ask is, "What happens if we don't, and they stay?"

Interestingly, reasons for growth and development appear to be trending up over time, and reasons related to being promoted or internal advancement appear to be trending down. Reasons for school also appear to be trending down, slightly.

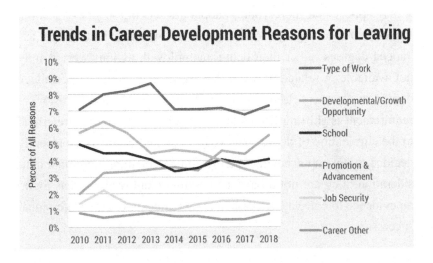

Trends in Career Development Reasons for Leaving

22% Quit for Career Development Reasons

Type of Work	33.1%
Lack of Growth and Development Opportunities	24.6%
Returning to School	18.4%
No Advancement or Promotional Opportunity	14%
Job Security	6.5%
General Career Reason	3.4%

The following examples are direct quotes from employees who voluntarily quit their organizations. These examples were pulled from exit interviews conducted across varied industries, including health care, automotive, retail, technology, financial services, manufacturing, and energy.

Type of Work

- "I just received a different opportunity. I was offered a change in work."

- "I was looking for a change in the industry. I need a career change after twenty-five years."

- "I wanted to try something different because I had done the same job in the department for ten years. I actually left my current job to take a lower-paying job because I wanted a different job so badly."

- "I received a better opportunity. I am able to do something different, as far as work goes."

- "I left because I wanted to pursue a different career."

Lack of Growth and Development Opportunities
- "I did not feel like I was learning or growing with the company."
- "I had no growth opportunities available, and that was discouraging. I was trying to get into a different department and was told I had to have experience first."
- "I left for a better growth opportunity. I am [now] able to use my skills."

Returning to School
- "I left because I wanted to go back to school."
- "I am back in grad school, and it is a full-time commitment."
- "I left to be able to focus on school."
- "I left because I went back to school part-time. I was having trouble going to school and work."
- "I left because I wanted to further my education. I felt that I needed more education to grow."

No Advancement or Promotional Opportunity
- "There was no room for me to move up."
- "I did not feel like I was able to move up. It felt like a dead-end job."

Job Security
- "I left the company because I did not feel like there was good job-security. There were nine layoffs while I was there."
- "I did not feel like my job was secure in the long term."

General Career Reason

- "I left because I made a personal decision to open my own business."

Work-life balance: In 2018, reasons that could be categorized under the work-life balance theme accounted for 12 percent of the reasons employees left (down from 13 percent in 2017). While work-life balance issues do not appear to be likely to overtake career development, reasons regarding commute (e.g., "I left because of the long commute, and that was my only reason for leaving the company."); schedule flexibility (e.g., "I left because I wanted to go to a different shift. I preferred the day shift. I was on nights for a long time."); travel (e.g., "I left the company because there was too much travel in the position that I was in," or "I left to seek another job. I wanted to travel."); and other work-life balance issues are appearing more frequently as the economy recovers. This reason theme accounted for a little less than 10 percent of reasons between 2010 and 2013, but increased in the past five years.

Trends in Work-Life Balance Reasons for Leaving

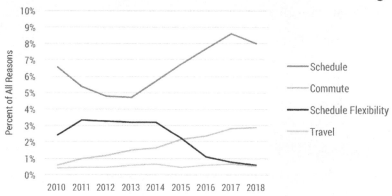

Within the work-life balance category, scheduling was the most important reason for leaving in 2018. Scheduling issues are a driving force behind why the work-life balance theme appears to have such an impact.

12% Quit for Work-Life Balance Reasons

Schedule	66.5%
Commute	24.6%
Schedule Flexibility	4.8%
Travel	4.2%

Schedule
- "I wanted to spend more time with family."
- "I was not getting enough hours."
- "I left the company because I already have a full-time job, and I was too busy to handle both schedules."
- "I needed a break. I needed some time off, and I did not think they would give me a leave of absence."
- "I was told that I could take a vacation. I booked my vacation and then found out that I was not approved by the time of it."
- "I asked if I could work from home, but they would not let me. I recently had a baby and needed to work remotely, but they changed their policy with that recently, and I was not able to do it."

Commute
- "The commute was not working out for me."
- "I started when I was supposed to work at a specific location. Soon after, I was asked to go to another location that was an additional forty minutes away."

- "I got a job that was closer to home. The drive was too far for me before."

- "I found another job that was closer to my home. This made it easier to take care of my kids."

- "I left because of the long commute, and that was my only reason for leaving the company."

Schedule Flexibility

- "I left because I wanted to go to a different shift. I preferred the day shift. I was on nights for a long time."

- "I am a college student, and I was told that I needed to be more flexible with my college schedule, not the other way around. I could not do that, so I left."

- "I had another full-time job, and I could not do both. I asked for part-time work, and they did not have anything to offer me."

- "I am expecting my second child. I got a job with more flexibility."

- "I left because I had a family emergency and was not able to switch to part time."

Travel

- "I left the company because there was too much travel in the position that I was in."

- "I did not like the road travel. I was on the road every day, covering for someone."

- "I left to seek another job. I wanted to travel."

Manager behavior was the third-largest theme for why people quit in 2018, accounting for more than eleven out of one hundred quit reasons. Reviewing the trends from 2010 through 2018, employees are increasingly leaving organizations due to management behavior. Some examples include general management behavior (e.g., "I left because I had a [manager] that was terrible to work for."); lack of professionalism (e.g., "[My bosses] show a lot of favoritism to their friends at work."); failing to support employees (e.g., "My coworkers and I were not getting along well. I did not feel my manager was handling it properly."); and poor communication (e.g., "Severe lack of transparency with leadership.").

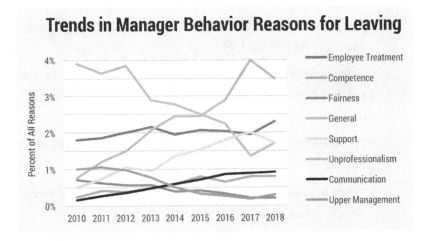

Trends in Manager Behavior Reasons for Leaving

Data do not support the adage "People don't quit their jobs; they quit their boss." Only about one in ten people said that problems with management was the most important reason for leaving. Neither do the data support the popular but erroneous notion that younger people quit because of their bosses more frequently than other age groups.

Increasing the rating of a supervisor from "very good" to "excellent" doubles the odds that the employee will report intent to stay with the company for a long time.

In 2017, when asked to rate their bosses in a stay interview, employees cited "professionalism" more than twice as much as "communication" or "competency." Of those who quit, unprofessionalism was cited almost four times more often than communication. Professionalism included having a professional demeanor and being helpful and supportive. Competency referred to leadership skills and included job-related knowledge. Communication included being available, having listening skills, and displaying clarity of expectations. While in general there are no differences across age or gender of why people choose to leave organizations, more women cite management-related reasons as important when deciding to leave.

11% Quit for Manager Behavior Reasons

Unprofessionalism	35.1%
Lack of Support	17.6%
Poor Employee Treatment	17.2%
General Behavior	11.8%
Poor Communication	7.7%
Lack of Manager Competence	7.1%
Manager Fairness	1.8%

Unprofessionalism
- "I left because the management was not professional. My supervisor and upper management were buddies and went on vacations together. The staff could never go to upper management with issues."

- "My supervisor was using inappropriate language and generally being abusive."

- "I could not deal with how my manager treated us in the field. He would yell at us in public. He was unprofessional."

Lack of Support
- "I did not feel supported by my manager."

- "The management structure did not fit well with the way that I work and find myself being able to thrive. There was just a lack of support, and many managers were too busy looking over my shoulder."

- "My supervisor never stood up for her team."

Poor Treatment of Employees
- "I left because I was treated poorly by management."

- "I left because the new director that was taking over had been our manager prior, and he was extremely disrespectful."

- "I felt like I was not treated well by the management. They did not talk to me in a constructive way. I was shown no respect."

General Behavior
- "It was like pure chaos all the time. Management did not get along. There is no structure at all. One manager would say one thing, and the other one would say something else."

- "I did not get along well with the district manager, and this caused some tension."

Poor Communication
- "Communication with department managers was somewhat challenging. I never met or heard from my direct manager at any time during my onboarding process."

- "I felt the communication was very poor at this branch, especially with scheduling."

Lack of Manager Competence

- "I did not think I had great support from leadership. My manager kept telling me I was doing a bad job and that I was not doing what I should be doing. Yet she would not tell me what I needed to do to improve."

Manager Fairness

- "There was a lack of consistency among the management."

- "I felt like there was a lot of favoritism from the management team."

- "I left because it was becoming difficult to work there. Some of the practices were unfair. I felt that night shift was treated differently by the management in terms of fairness."

Upper Management

- "I did not like the upper leadership. I felt like they did not care about the employees. They did not listen to us."

- "I left the company because I lost confidence within upper management in how they were operating the company."

Compensation and benefits appeared as the fourth most frequently occurring theme in 2018 (up from fifth in 2017) and accounted for 9.6 percent of the reasons employees left.

Trends in Compensation and Benefits Reasons for Leaving

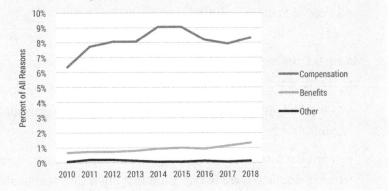

Wage growth lagged during the economic recovery. As the US emerged from the recession, pay did not increase at the same rate as job openings or job growth, until recently. This is clearly a time of transition and ambivalence as employers are both spending cautiously and recognizing the need to reevaluate pay based on fairness, social pressure, competitiveness, retention, and cost-of-living requirements.

Regardless, employers must also be cautious of pay inflation, thinking raises in compensation solve all problems. While compensation represents 85.8 percent of the compensation and benefits category of reasons, compensation as a reason alone represents just over 9 percent of all reasons for leaving. This conflicts with many of the claims about causes of turnover in the media and by other research organizations reporting largely from flawed methodologies and biases that drive many self-promoting research studies.

10% Quit for Compensation and Benefits Reasons

Compensation	85.8%
Benefits	13.4%
Other	0.8%

Compensation

- "I was treated unfairly. I had been there over eight years, and I never got a raise."

- "I left because I felt as though I was significantly underpaid in my position as a senior staff."

- "I left because I went to HR two years ago because I found out that new employees were getting paid more than I was. I had been with the company for more than ten years, so I started looking for a new job."

- "The key issue that I was having was inadequate compensation relative to the demands of the job and the marketplace."

Benefits

- "I left because I found a job that offered a pension plan. I did not get that there."

- "After thirty-eight years working for [my company], this past April, they decided to remove the benefits, so I decided to retire."

- "I found a job that offered better benefits. There is a better tuition reimbursement, and there is also better medical. I do not have to jump through hoops to get the bills paid."

Well-being includes personal reasons for leaving an organization related to physical or mental health concerns of the employee or those of his or her family. This theme accounts for over 8 percent of all responses given by employees, which makes it the fifth-largest theme.

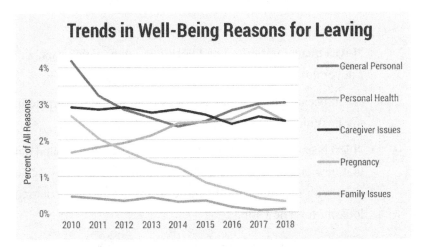

Trends in Well-Being Reasons for Leaving

Since 2010, well-being reasons for leaving have declined from 12 percent. As marketplace conditions have improved, employees have found opportunities to prioritize caring for themselves and their families and will continue to place high importance on these reasons for leaving. It is also likely that at least some of the efforts companies have made to promote general health have had a small, but noteworthy, impact.

Some companies are addressing maternity and paternity leave. *The Wall Street Journal* cited, "Employers such as American Express say actively promoting paternity-leave policies also gives them an edge in recruiting top talent."[25] American Express encourages its employees to take advantage of these benefits by hanging posters of dads cradling babies that read, "Take up to 20 weeks paternity leave. You both deserve it."[26]

One-third of employees surveyed cited general personal reasons as the most important reason for leaving in this category, at 35.6 percent. Examples of general personal reasons for leaving include the need to resolve personal problems, the desire to spend more time with family, and the need for a less stressful job.

Personal health reasons for leaving accounted for nearly one-third of well-being reasons for leaving, at 30.1 percent. Employees who cited personal health issues mentioned medical issues that temporarily or permanently prevented them from working the required hours. Less frequent but additional reasons for leaving included pregnancy and family issues.

Caregiver issues is the third most cited well-being reason for leaving, at 29.7 percent. The preference to care for a child and the need to care for an ill or aged family member are examples of caregiver issues that were cited.

Employers who do not actively pay attention to their workers' needs to take care of themselves and their families will likely see turnover. To ensure you keep good employees as long as possible, it's critical to understand the challenges that employees face and to work with them to accommodate special needs in a reasonable manner.

8% Quit for Well-Being Reasons

General Personal	35.6%
Personal Health	30.1%
Caregiver Issues	29.7%
Pregnancy	3.9%
Family Issues	0.8%

General Personal
- "I left so I could work days until my deployment. I was working overnight, and I needed to spend time with family, so it was just a better schedule where I could come home after work and spend the evening with everyone."

- "Based on my own prioritizing of my life, something was going on that I needed to take care of."

- "I am leaving for personal reasons that I would rather not discuss."

- "I left because I decided to take personal time off and not work for a little while."

Personal Health

- "I was looking for a different environment. I had medical issues and could not be on my feet thirteen hours a day. I have arthritis. I found another job that would let me have a better mix of desk- and non-desk-job duties."

- "I am having personal health issues that are non-work related."

- "I had back surgery, and felt I was not able to perform the job duties anymore."

Caregiver Issues

- "I left the company because my father was in the hospital and I had to care for him before he passed."

- "At this moment I cannot work full time and take care of my children."

- "I had some medical issues with my mother. I am her oldest child, so I had to take off to help her."

- "I am a single mom, and the hours were rough for me to find a babysitter."

Pregnancy

- "I am having a high-risk pregnancy, so I cannot work."

- "I had a baby and I could no longer afford the childcare."
- "I am seven months pregnant, and the demands of the job were getting to be too much."

Family Issues
- "I had personal issues in my family."
- "I left because my family was having issues and I needed to be with them to help get them resolved."
- "I left because I had a family situation, and I was not able to get any more time off."

Job characteristics accounted for 8.1 percent of reasons for leaving in 2018, as employees cited an unmanageable workload, a lack of enjoyment, ill preparation, and a lack of ownership as reasons for leaving. While toward the bottom of the list of categories of reasons, the job characteristics category has increased by 130 percent over the past eight years, up from 3 percent in 2010. As job options have increased, workers are not tolerant of jobs that do not meet their expectations.

Trends in Job Characteristics Reasons for Leaving

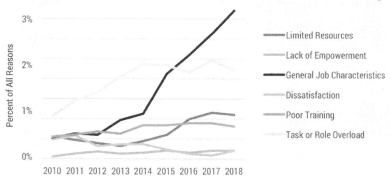

General job characteristics caused by aspects of the job represented the largest reason in this category, at 45.7 percent. However, this doesn't necessarily mean that employees want less to do. Employees who cited general job characteristics as the main reason for leaving explained they were not offered positions with more flexibility in how they accomplished their work, or they did not feel they had a voice, or they wanted to be challenged, or they simply didn't enjoy the job or find it meaningful.

Employees who felt overloaded with work or experienced a high level of stress in their jobs represented nearly one-third (26.7 percent) of reasons for leaving in the job characteristics category. Unacceptable workloads, as perceived by employees, could have been caused by a lack of clear expectations or by an increase in work caused by record job openings, or the continued flattening of middle-management attention. This is a critical point to understand. Turnover can lead to more turnover as workers who remain often pick up the slack, which often leads to increased dissatisfaction.

Adequate tools, information, proper training, and attention are also important to employees. More than 13 percent of reasons in the job characteristics category were attributed to limited resources, where employees stated that they were hindered from doing a job when they were not provided adequate resources. Poor training accounted for 9.6 percent, where employees stated that their jobs became difficult because they were not properly trained on technology or systems.

Employers must evaluate and be confident that they are creating realistic job previews, communicating core tasks, and providing effective training to prevent turnover.

8% Quit for Job Characteristics Reasons

General Job Characteristics	45.7%
Task or Role Overload	26.7%
Limited Resources	13.5%
Poorly Trained	9.6%
Lack of Empowerment	2.4%
Dissatisfied with Work	2.1%

General Job Characteristics

- "I did not like the job. I felt like a telemarketer."

- "They had me working about thirteen hours a week."

- "I went back to a former employer. I have more autonomy here."

- "I am a software engineer, and I like to be challenged. There just was not enough work for me to do. Also, the work was not technically challenging. We were not using the latest technology."

Task or Role Overload

- "I was way too stressed out, to the point I got depressed. I could not handle all of the stress they were piling on."

- "I left the company because the job was very stressful. I felt like I could not handle the workload that I was doing."

Limited Resources

- "The job expectations did not match up to what was said in the interview. They told me that I was going to have the tools to provide excellent care. I did not have all the tools to help all of my customers."

- "Organization is severely understaffed, which creates additional stress and workload for those who work hardest."

- "I did not feel like the goals were attainable. I was stressed out and needed to quit."

Poorly Trained
- "They did not provide me with adequate orientation for the documentation that they require. The orientation had to be done on tablet, and I did not get the support necessary to complete it."

- "I left because the training was not enough to keep us up on the regular changes."

- "I did not feel that they gave me the proper training for the position that I was offered, and that made my job difficult on a daily basis."

- "I was written up for relying too heavily on my teammates. The technology was new to me for this job. I was not properly trained on how to use them. I should have been trained instead of written up."

Lack of Empowerment
- "I left because I felt that I was invisible and did not have a voice."

Dissatisfied with Work
- "I left because I was not really satisfied there. I was not really big on sitting in a cubicle all day."

- "I left because I was not satisfied with my job. I did not like the kind of work I was doing."

Work environment reasons represented more than 5 percent of the reasons employees left their jobs in 2018. While the lowest-ranked controllable category, work environment reasons have trended up. As employees become dissatisfied with current workplace conditions, they have increasingly taken opportunities to work in a climate with coworkers whom they prefer.

Trends in Work Environment Reasons for Leaving

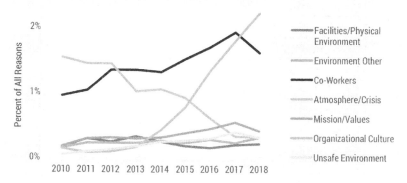

Culture does matter. Culture-employee misfit was the top work-environment-related reason employees quit last year, as 41 percent of employees cited this as the most important categorical reason for leaving. Employees who left for culture issues frequently cited widespread unprofessional behavior and personality differences that did not match their preferred working conditions.

Problematic coworkers was second at 30.3 percent in this theme. Harassment by a coworker, teams that did not mesh well, general bad attitudes, and lack of issue resolution were cited under problematic coworkers. The importance of coworker relationships must not be underestimated. Current employees who rated their employer as "excellent" cited their coworkers as the driving factor of their rating.

Mission or values accounted for 8.2 percent of reasons in the work environment category of reasons. This included perceptions of unethical behavior on behalf of the organization and personal values that did not match that of the organization. Safety issues (7 percent), a hostile atmosphere or crisis (6 percent), poor facilities, and other conditions accounted for the remainder of reasons within the work environment category.

5% Quit for Work Environment Reasons

Culture/Employee Not a Fit	41%
Problematic Coworkers	30.3%
Problem with Mission or Values	8.2%
Environment Other	5.9%
Unsafe Environment	5.7%
Hostile Atmosphere or Organizational Crises	4.9%
Poor Facilities	4%

Culture/Employee Not a Fit
- "I did not like the culture there. It was very political."
- "It seemed like a lazy [or] sleepy environment, no energy."
- "There were no incentives to stay late [or] work hard."

Problematic Coworkers
- "I had a problem with some people that I made management aware of, but nothing ever came of it."
- "I transferred to [my new unit] and some of the key nurses at that facility made me feel unappreciated and that I did not do anything right."
- "The staff did not work cohesively. We did not mesh well at all."

- "I felt that the culture was not very professional because there were employees who were very rude."

Problem with Mission or Values
- "I left because the core values were no longer in alignment with my own."
- "It was not the right environment for me anymore. The leadership was frequently changing the vision and direction of the organization."
- "I did not like the way things were run. It seemed that there were more concerns about money than the well-being of the employees."
- "I think it is an unethical company. It is not a transparent company when it comes to pay."

Environment Other
- "The work environment was always very negative."
- "I could not handle working inside anymore."
- "I did not feel the setting was right for me."

Unsafe Environment
- "I left because I had safety concerns."
- "I left the company because I reported some issues about safety regarding smelling alcohol on [a supervisor's] breath. . . . nothing was ever done about it."
- "I felt like it was a dangerous job."
- "I felt that safety was no longer a concern of the company."

Hostile Atmosphere or Organizational Crises
- "I did not agree with their policies in relation to the way that I was asked to do my job. There were some ethical and legal issues that they were not addressing."
- "I left because I was being harassed by another colleague."

Poor Facilities
- "I got stuck in the elevator three times while working with the company. The elevator was pitch black, and they never fixed it."

Employees will define the workplace conditions that drive satisfaction and commitment.

Work environment, while ranked low, has trended up, which shows that employers are not doing enough to understand and improve conditions that could prevent turnover. Although a lesser-cited reason for leaving, conditions related to the work environment are more controllable than other factors. Fix the elevator already.

TURNOVER COSTS ARE RISING

Employers know turnover is expensive. Just how expensive is arguable, but any turnover cost is real and can be reduced. According to the Bureau of Labor Statistics, the median wage for forty-hour-per-week workers in the United States is $44,564 per year.[27] Based on a conservative cost of turnover at $15,000 per employee, the total cost of turnover for US companies in 2018 was $617 billion. Based on a 77 percent voluntary quit rate, the controllable cost for US companies is $475 billion.

- Reducing preventable turnover by 10 percent would save $47.5 billion.

- Reducing preventable turnover by 50 percent would save $237 billion.

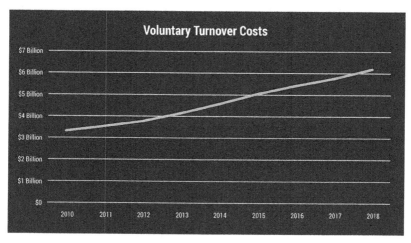

Based on a review of over 34,000 employees who exited their employers in 2016, the most important reasons for leaving were identified and costed. When inserting and utilizing data unique to a specific employer, this information can provide actionable direction, identify ROI, and evaluate the effectiveness of specific interventions.[28]

Total US Cost Per Exit Factor in 2016

Factor	Frequency*	Percentage	Cost
Career Development	7024	20%	$105,360,000.00
Work-Life Balance	4373	13%	$65,595,000.00
Management Behavior	3908	11%	$58,620,000.00
Compensation & Benefits	3126	9%	$46,890,000.00
Relocation	3111	9%	$46,665,000.00
Well-Being	3073	9%	$46,095,000.00
Job Characteristics	2725	8%	$40,875,000.00
Involuntary	2563	8%	$38,445,000.00
Retirement	2314	7%	$34,710,000.00
Workplace Environment	2161	6%	$32,415,000.00
Total	34378	100%	$143,805,000.00

The ability to contain turnover costs is not only a competitive advantage, it is now necessary in today's employee-in-control marketplace to retain and build profits.

Considering the median US worker, a one-hundred-thousand-dollar investment in retention will pay for itself if it prevents seven employees from leaving.

GENERATIONAL MYTHOLOGIES MARGINALIZE EMPLOYEES

Seldom does a conversation about employee engagement or turnover not eventually land on the topic of generational concerns. Millennials are taking the brunt of this discussion, and too few point out the fallacies present in the assumptions being made.

Rather than rely on popular generational differences, career stage explains much more about why employees leave employers.

The reasons for leaving within age groups are no surprise; they are the typical reasons for leaving that individuals in these age groups have given for decades. Younger workers have been more focused on jumpstarting their careers, and older workers have been more focused on retirement.

Younger workers, ages eighteen to twenty-four, leave for reasons that are typical for workers at this stage of life, who are new to the workforce and at the beginning of their careers. The top category of reasons for leaving among this age group is career development at 28.3 percent. Within this category, returning to school was the leading reason. The relocation category took second place at 13.8 percent, with work-life balance following third at 12.9 percent. Young people are long-term focused, trying to figure out what they do and do not like doing, and they are more mobile than other age groups due to their life stage.

Workers in the middle of their careers, ages twenty-five to fifty-four, often leave as they progress through various life stages, and the reasons for leaving reflect this theory. Career development was the top category of reasons for this age group at 21.2 percent. Within this category, type of work was the top reason. Manager behavior was the second most cited reason for this age group, at 14.4 percent. Work-life balance was close to 14 percent. Many individuals in this age group are in the prime of their career growth, as they have been for decades, and today's marketplace is providing many opportunities for them to grow or advance.

Older workers, ages fifty-five and older, are in a different life stage and are looking toward retirement. Retirement was the leading category of reasons for this group to leave their jobs, at 29 percent. Manager behavior ranked as the second category of reasons, and well-being ranked third. This is typical, as workers are less inclined to relocate or change jobs at this stage of their lives. These workers care less about career and pay; however, they are concerned about their personal health and want to be treated with respect.

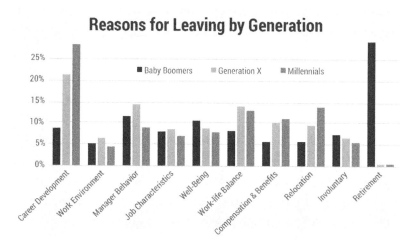

Reasons for Leaving by Generation

REASONS FOR STAYING ARE DIFFERENT THAN REASONS FOR LEAVING

It is as important to understand the reasons people stay as it is to understand why they leave, and these reasons aren't always the same. Workplace conditions that cause job satisfaction are different from the conditions that cause dissatisfaction.[29] Factors related to the work itself that bring a sense of fulfillment have been found to drive satisfaction and retention when they are high. Factors like pay and manager behavior lead to dissatisfaction and turnover when they are lacking. To optimize retention, the employer must understand the interplay and address both satisfying and dissatisfying factors.

Given data from stay studies with employees still in their organization, an employer can capture and categorize specific reasons employees intend to stay for a given length of time. For example, employees who only plan to stay for three months cite different reasons than those who plan on staying for one year. To find the real reasons for staying, the Work Institute studied the most important reasons given by employees who said they plan to stay for "a long time."

The most common reasons for staying were career development, job characteristics, and work environment. Interviews from those who exited showed job characteristics and work environment as lower-ranking reasons for leaving—sixth and seventh on the list. Work-life balance and management behavior ranked second and third in reasons for leaving, but aren't as important to how employees foresee staying with a company. This is in line with the research that says reasons for satisfaction are different from reasons for dissatisfaction.

Understanding those who stay is as important as understanding those who exit. Looking at just one of these pieces of information tells only part of the story.

Top Reasons for Staying are Different from Top Reasons for Leaving

TOP REASONS FOR STAYING	TOP REASONS FOR LEAVING
Career Development	Career Development
Job Characteristics	Work-Life Balance
Work Environment	Management Behavior
Compensation & Benefits	Compensation & Benefits
Work-Life Balance	Well-Being
Management Behavior	Retirement
Retirement	Relocation
	Involuntary
	Job Characteristics
	Work Environment

Employees really can expect more from employers as their job options increase. Too, employers can keep more people longer, supporting competitiveness and growth, if they choose to. As previously stated, 42 million US employees voluntarily left their employers (excluding retirements and relocations) in 2017, and 77 percent of the most important reasons former employees left were preventable by the employer. [30]

Three out of four employees who quit last year would have stayed if easily preventable issues had been addressed.

The categories of reasons for quitting have not shifted significantly in the past several years. Clearly, employers have been slow to respond to changing workforce requirements, ignoring retention opportunities, or intervening in the wrong areas. Turnover continues to rise, causing harm to companies.

Preventable reasons for turnover, reasons that companies are ignoring, also continue to rise. Employers have a choice to accurately identify workplace conditions that need to change and make the changes, or continue to lose the people necessary to do the work that needs to be done.

Preventable Turnover 2014-2017

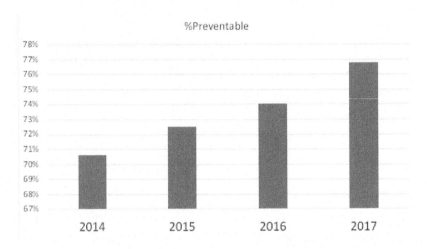

COMPANIES MUST BE ENGAGED

While hiring and selection is important, oftentimes organizations place more emphasis on finding the people who fit the workplace as opposed to shaping the workplace to fit the best people. Each part of the employment process, from hiring and training to leadership development, requires a greater emphasis on becoming an Engaged EmployER. Employee perceptions are developed throughout the employment life cycle, from the moment employees begin to interact with the company to the moment they leave.

In an economy where employees are in control, companies can't afford to ignore workforce opinions on specific actions that attract and keep workers.

Organizations must give their employees a voice.

Employers must trust that employees will share what needs to happen in the organization. Employee studies from the 1940s into the Quality Circle studies of the 1980s to more current studies repeatedly demonstrate the value of total employee participation.[31] Employees will report what practices are needed in their organization—when, where, and with whom. Ask, hear, acknowledge, thank them for their input, and do something to effect necessary changes. As beneficial to the employee and the organization, evaluate whether additional change interventions are needed by again asking, hearing, acknowledging, and thanking them for input. Then repeat.

Quite simply, reciprocal communication channels between company and worker, in which a company is soliciting and listening to feedback from employees, will bring out meaningful insights.

Workers will report keen insights into strengths and identify where improvements are needed—if and when employers ask in the right way and respond.

THREE

WORKPLACE MYTHOLOGY, MISTAKES, AND OPPORTUNITY

It ain't so much the things you don't know that get you into
trouble. It's the things you know that just ain't so.
—Arthur Ward (1834–1867)

To reduce costs associated with disengagement and turnover, RAI
(Renal Advantage Inc.) conducted a baseline survey with its entire
employee population. RAI needed to know the preferences, expecta-
tions, and intents of its workforce. Keeping their finger on the pulse
of the workforce provided RAI management and supervisors with the
opportunity to address disengagement before employees walked out
the door.

RAI focused on three key areas for improvement: the perception
of RAI as an employer, the quality of supervisor performance, and
overall turnover. After obtaining the results, all supervisors were ini-
tially made responsible for implementing changes with the objective

to lower "fair"/"poor" responses to below 15 percent and raise "excellent" responses to above 30 percent.

Since the dawn of the industrial age until the late 1990s, most companies were in control of the employment relationship. Employees went to work for a company, laboring at the pleasure of the employer. Many were harnessed to an employer due to pension and health-insurance restrictions. Outlier employers created environments that fostered employment relationships workers valued. Others created conditions workers were forced to tolerate. Some companies created conditions that led workers to affiliate with outside organizations, such as unions, associations, and other social organizations that fulfilled employees' preferences for community.

Then a shift happened. Downsizings and the headline-making layoffs violated legacy promises and expectations of lifelong employment. Notably for the workforce, retirement plans and health insurance became portable, thus freeing employment choices. Employees came to realize they were no longer dependent on a single employer to fulfill a lifelong employment contract, and they could manage their careers differently. This newly liberated employee population, this emerging workforce, recognized a way to achieve career satisfaction and opportunity by finding opportunities with other, more preferable employers.

Work continues to transition from an employer-in-control to an employee-in-control environment. This transition defines an employee population whose attitudes and preferences differ from the workforce of the past. As employees have choices, they can leverage their knowledge and skills with organizational conditions that suit them.

Still, some companies continue to believe that employees are merely commodities to be traded or replaced, or that employees are dependent on the employer for livelihood. In some high-unemployment geographies, this may be particularly true. Increasingly, however, companies are coming to terms with the fact that a restricted job opportunity market is ending. High unemployment in the post-2008-recession years may have relaxed attention to employee relationship requirements, but those days have ended or are numbered. Today, an employer must listen for, know, and attend to differing preferences, expectations, and intents of employees.

Employers who ignore this evolving employee-in-control dynamic will lose.

The December 2018 jobs report from the Bureau of Labor Statistics showed that the economy entered 2019 with positive momentum for continued growth, while employers entered with mounting challenges to fill jobs. Throughout 2019, the unemployment rate dipped below 4 percent, the labor force participation rate was relatively stagnant at 62 percent, and the job openings rate balanced around 3.6 percent. This loudly signaled that the number of available workers was flat while the number of jobs was growing. Workers learned they had options. The number of open jobs continued to increase throughout 2019, and the additional demand for workers continued.

Employers attempted to capitalize on growth opportunity by adding jobs. However, the workers were not to be had. Unemployment remained at near-record lows, the number of workers entering the workforce decreased, and the labor participation rate remained unchanged. The increased demand (and stagnant supply) neared 2006 levels and even approached 2001 levels, when it was the highest recorded by the Bureau of Labor Statistics. In the immortalized language of Yogi Berra, "It's like déjà vu all over again."

The quit rate, which can be viewed as a measure of workers' willingness and ability to change jobs, has risen, but not as dramatically as unemployment has declined. If the supply of workers continues to be stagnant, the quit rate will have nowhere to go but up. Employers will continue to face challenges to fill the jobs needed to grow their business and will have few options but to change their efforts to find and keep workers.

In a real estate market where the buyer has the advantage, we invoke buyers'-market strategies and tactics. Alternatively, where the seller has the advantage, we reference sellers'-market behaviors. In an employment market, where there are more jobs than people, we need to acknowledge an employees'-advantage market.

Core to adjusting to the current employee-in-control market is stamping out the employer-in-control perspective that drives management strategy and tactics representative of times past. This section presents some key management errors and questionable practices, indicative of companies that may still not recognize the need to adapt to today's employee-in-control environment. To win, today's employer needs to adopt an EmployER Engagement philosophy and practice.

STOP AND THINK

A manager's view of employees is sometimes shaped by assumptions about roles. The way we view our and others' roles and make judgements about them directs our behavior.

What do you believe is the difference between a manager perspective and an employee perspective?

Think of the differences on a day-to-day basis. How do a manager's beliefs affect an employee's overall engagement and intent to stay?

Consider this: They are not your employees. You are their employer. Does this shift your thinking? How?

"One of the biggest mistakes a company can make is blindly adopting the latest HR fad without tailoring it to the organization's unique orientation."
—Deloitte & Touche, Human Capital ROI Study: Creating Shareholder Value through People

QUIT DEPENDING ON OTHERS' BEST PRACTICES

"Best practices" came into the management lexicon to identify and implement processes, systems, and behaviors that should produce the best results. Gaining popularity during the quality movement of the early 1990s, best practices were especially relevant for International Organization for Standardization (ISO) certification.

Best practices work—only when they do. For example, replicating practices for complying with accounting, ethical, or legal requirements may make sense. Likewise, replicating procedures for machine maintenance may be valuable if equipment is standard and functioning is predictable. A best practice may be to change oil every five thousand miles, calibrate instrumentation monthly, and back up data daily.

Where best practices often fail, however, is in situations where the conditions under which equipment is operating vary. For example, given different weather conditions or altitudes, others' practices for lubrication may need to be adjusted and the practice for maintaining tire pressure may need to change.

It's the conditions or the context which often cause others' practices to no longer be sufficient, let alone "best." While the American Medical Association may recommend cholesterol screening and treatment as key to the annual physical, everyone does not need to be prescribed lipid-lowering drugs. The patient with a compromised liver or poor eating and exercise behaviors may benefit from alternative treatment. Best practices work when conditions are constant. Of critical note, though, companies are not constant nor do they operate in the same context. Neither are people standard pieces of equipment with stable, unvarying, and predictable functioning.

Yet employers are bombarded with the promises of others' best practices. The recognition companies are promising to reduce turnover if you just give out their dimensional reward and recognition products. Other promises are made by the benefits companies, if only you would offer their enhanced program. The test publishing companies promise that you too can have an engaged workforce if you just use their selection and development assessments.

Almost all companies are unique, even within industries. Rather than depending on others' best practices, employers need only to look within to develop engagement and retention.

Let's go to the facts. The chances of your company's having the most common turnover profile are less than 8 percent.[32] Across 173 companies researched in 2016 and looking at all possible combinations of the top reasons employees cited for leaving, results revealed that only 7 percent of companies shared the most common turnover profile. This fact alone emphasizes the need for employers to understand reasons for leaving within their company's unique workforce, work environment conditions, geography, and work context.

Companies are incredibly diverse in the reasons employees leave. A common turnover profile does not exist.

Across organizations, 86 percent of companies had career development in their top three reasons for leaving. Reasons related to work-life balance, management behavior, and compensation and benefits were among the top three reasons for leaving for only 30–40 percent of companies. Forty-eight percent of companies share career as the top theme. The reasons within each theme vary dramatically depending on the organization. While one hospital may have employees leaving primarily because of task or role overload (job characteristics) and work schedule (work-life balance), another hospital may have more employees quit because of lack of training (job characteristics) and commute (work-life balance).

Observe the difference among and between survey results:

- For Company X, 23 percent of turnover was due to relocation, 20 percent was retirement, 17 percent was management behavior, and less than 1 percent of turnover was due to job characteristics. However, for Company Y, 41 percent of turnover was due to job characteristics, and 24 percent was due to compensation and benefits.

- For Company Z, 3 percent of turnover was due to compensation and benefits, while 20 percent was involuntary, and 12 percent was due to career development.

- Career development was the largest theme for eighty clients and did not occur or was in the bottom three reasons for thirteen clients.

- Relocation was the largest theme for twelve clients and did not occur or was in the bottom three reasons for sixty-nine clients.

- Work-life balance was the largest theme for fifteen clients and did not occur or was in the bottom three reasons for forty-one clients.

- Personal was the largest theme for five clients and did not occur or was in the bottom three reasons for eighty clients.

- Involuntary was the largest theme for eighteen clients and did not occur or was in the bottom three reasons for 112 clients.

- Management was the largest theme for eight clients and did not occur or was in the bottom three reasons for fifty clients.

- Retirement was the largest theme for ten clients and did not occur or was in the bottom three reasons for 111 clients.

- Compensation and benefits was the largest theme for four clients and did not occur or was in the bottom three reasons for sixty-eight clients.

- Environment was the largest theme for zero clients and did not occur or was in the bottom three reasons for 132 clients.

- Job characteristics was the largest theme for one client and did not occur or was in the bottom three reasons for 93 clients.

Why is it that companies want to copy others' engagement and retention practices? Just because a program was successful in a western-region hospital does not mean success is replicated in the middle-America corporate office. Employees, unemployment rates, community and economic development commitments, traffic, and organizational resources are independent variables. Treating them as if they are constant is an error.

Rather than defaulting to copying others' best practices, employers must know the whats and whys of engagement and retention and what is needed to improve the employer-employee relationship, the organization's brand, and increased productivity. Employers must remain wary of jumping on the latest engagement management bandwagon. As others' best practices are pitched as a solution, exercise caution.

Best practices come from within.

Using employee turnover as an example, quantifying an organization's top reasons for leaving and identifying the prevailing themes of attraction, intent to stay, and turnover are important. Organizations differ in customers, mission, culture, geography, unemployment rate, commute, and management behavior, within and between. Each organization has its own unique combination of challenges. Implementing others' best practices can have unintended side effects, especially if those practices don't address the real problem. Organizations can save money, time, frustration, and employees by measuring, developing, and intervening with their own best practices.

"Some are born great, some achieve greatness, and some hire public relations officers."
—Daniel J. Boorstin

SPINNING WITH BENCHMARKS

Many companies chase benchmarks. For some reason they want to know vacancy levels, turnover percentages, and turnover reasons of other employers.

I recall too many conversations with HR professionals who expressed a certain amount of pride because their turnover was only 22 percent, when the reported industry average may have been 24 percent. Converting this (false) pride to dollars, assuming a thousand employees and using a conservative $15,000-per-employee turnover cost, what this HR person was telling us is that average industry turnover is $3.6 million while his turnover is only $3.3 million.

It's hard to celebrate turnover cost. Securing an internal turnover measure of 22 percent while the industry average is 24 percent does not mean the company is doing a good job. It means the company is losing $3.3 million. Regardless of the fact that one's error is not as big as another's, it remains an error.

—Thomas F. Mahan

While engagement-, retention-, and productivity-success-and-error rates might at first seem like the perfect fit for benchmarking data, it can be difficult to make valid comparisons. Others' best practices, differences in cultures, definitions of strengths and errors, employee preferences and expectations, and locations compromise an apples-to-apples comparison. Perhaps of greater importance, comparisons are of little value as there is no acceptable incidence rate for errors, or due to the absence of high-potential replacements, bad hires, or legal or ethical violations.

Organizations must work to minimize and eliminate errors, not just be slightly better than others.

Rather than keep up with how one's own organizational retention-and-engagement successes and failures compare to other companies, leaders who are serious about making positive developmental changes must focus on measuring and taking the actions necessary to increase their own strengths and decrease or eliminate their own errors.

When one international automotive company received their survey data on retention and engagement, their response was, "How do we compare with others in the industry?" Their primary concern was whether or not their data was favorable compared to competitors and if their own measures were in line with industry benchmarks. They were losing high potential engineers, yet they only cared whether they were worse than their competitors. They were losing 10 to 15 percent of their high potential candidates to a very specific issue that could have been simple to remedy. I continue to wonder if they would be sufficiently satisfied with defects coming off their assembly line, if the defect percentage was less than the competition.

—Danny A. Nelms

Contentment with being like others drives an organization to mediocrity, not excellence.

Comparisons with external or industry benchmarks merely provide information as to whether an employer is better than, worse than, or the same as others. The comparisons tell nothing about what a company needs to do with employees in its unique environment. Rather than attending to other employers' data, organizations must focus on their own internal intent-to-stay and intent-to-leave measures, and their own remediation and developmental requirements—those unique to their employee populations.

STOP AND THINK

What percentage of poor hiring decisions would be considered as unacceptable hiring performance?

What percentage of turnover would be acceptable?

How many sexual harassment claims are reasonable?

What percentage of the workforce intending to leave in the next quarter is acceptable?

MAKING ASSUMPTIONS ABOUT YOUR WORKFORCE

I recently listened to the noise of a self-proclaimed workforce expert, a 'life coach.' This breakfast presentation was offered to help executives know what they must attend to during this time of engagement, attraction, and retention challenges. The invitation included language such as 'critical to attend,' 'absolutely must attend,' and 'attend for the survival of your business.'

As time permits, I occasionally attend these meetings. It is often a good opportunity to share a cup of coffee with friends and colleagues, a time to renew relationships. I also know that while a presentation may cover forty-five to ninety minutes of content, I typically leave with a few thoughts worthy of additional exploration.

My most recent experience was not about learning something new. It was embarrassing. Instead I learned about ignorance. The presenter's recommendations were just plain wrong, and I fear for those managers at risk of acting on her recommendations. Turns out this workforce consultant is a self-proclaimed generational differences expert who would have us believe that she has uncovered some secret for managing categories of people born in certain years.

She suggested that each generation has some sort of idiosyncratic personality that we must all understand to effectively attract and engage them. For a fee, I am told that I too can have generational treasure maps and that these secrets will inform [me of] how to differently manage each age group.

—Thomas F. Mahan

Managerial decisions and subsequent actions derive from assumptions about people and how one views the world.

As behavior scientists, we are conflicted about the generational differences argument. While it is often presented in entertaining ways, and sometimes it even sounds like it could make sense, it doesn't really have any arms. Sure, workers in different age brackets may have different ways of doing things. They certainly have had different experiences. Data, however, just doesn't support the popular and generally held belief that younger employees have preferences, expectations, and intents that differ from other age groups. Possibly the most damaging effect of this approach is that it encourages anti-inclusive attitudes toward certain age groupings of employees.

Today, this is particularly true with popular conversations and attitudes about millennial populations. It's hard to open any workplace newsletter, human resource publication, or business newspaper without reading of the so-called millennial problem. Prejudice based on a person's age, from new workers and all the way through retirees, aside from creating risk for an organization, is just plain wrong. Similar judgements were held in the past about Generation X and baby boomers. Is it just a matter of time before we start marginalizing Gen Z, iGen, or centennials? Common stereotypes about employees are myths and marginalize people. A few known errors are offered:

Erroneous stereotype #1: *Women leave jobs for different reasons than men.*

When we take a closer look at gender in the context of life stage, we find that the reasons men and women leave are most different for workers in their twenties and become almost the same among employees in their forties and fifties.

Erroneous stereotype #2: *Different generations require different workforce strategies.*

Generational difference has received a lot of attention in the popular media. We are told that employees of certain ages are different, need to be managed differently, and need to be induced to behave based on age-specific reinforcers. We have been told we need to re-parent millennials, treating them as if they are children. While supporting the fact that employees of different age groups have had differing reactions to experiences, usually based on natural and normal developmental age responses, the professional press shows there are many more variations and meaningful differences within generations than between them.[33]

Assuming employees within generations require the same strategy could lead to wasted effort and ineffective initiatives. Ultimately, employees have unique points of view across and within ages. Generational stereotypes have limited usefulness and risk misguiding retention efforts.[34]

Rather than attend to generational differences, if reasons for leaving support it, employers should attend to career stage. Career was the largest theme for leaving for people ages sixteen to twenty-four, with relocation and work-life balance coming in second and third respectively. Employees who are twenty-five to fifty-four had career as the largest theme, with work-life balance coming in second, and management and relocation tied for third. For employees fifty-five years and older, retirement was the largest theme (arguably a career theme), well-being came in second, and management came in third.

Early in their careers, employees seek out training, want employers to be flexible with schedules, attempt to figure out who they are occupationally, and demonstrate willingness to relocate. Pay seems to be a relatively important reason as well. In the middle of their career, employees are looking for flexibility in their schedule, as well as better pay and benefits; they get pickier about the type of work they do and who supervises it; and they are still willing to relocate to find growth or better opportunities. In late career, employees are far more stable, meaning less likely to relocate. They are increasingly picky about their schedules and supervisor and want to be treated with respect.

Reasons for Leaving by Age Group

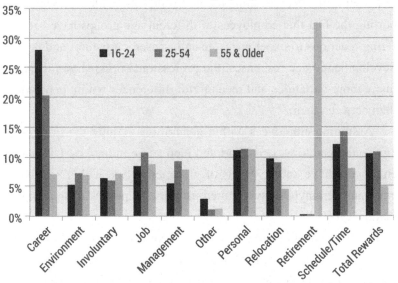

In 2017, employees ages sixteen to twenty-four reported the primary reason for quitting was school (17 percent), followed by scheduling reasons (11 percent), type of work (9 percent), employee-initiated relocation (9 percent), pay (8 percent), involuntary job elimination/reduction in force (4 percent), developmental/growth opportunity (3 percent), personal, job characteristics, and commute (each about 3 percent).

Employees twenty-five to fifty-four reported the primary reason for quitting as scheduling (10 percent), followed by pay (9 percent), type of work (8 percent), employee-initiated relocation (6 percent), developmental or growth opportunity (5 percent), unprofessional manager behavior (4 percent), job characteristics (3 percent), caregiver issues (3 percent), personal reasons (3 percent), and commute (3 percent).

Employees fifty-five and older reported the number one reason for quitting as retirement (32 percent). The next reasons were scheduling issues (6 percent), health (6 percent), pay (4 percent), involuntary job elimination/reduction in force (4 percent), unprofessional manager (4 percent), workload/stress, type of work, personal reasons, and employee-initiated relocation (about 3 percent each).

Management behavior becomes a larger factor as employees reach later stages in their careers. Prioritizing compensation and benefits increases toward the middle of the career cycle and decreases with age. Personal reasons, job characteristics, and workplace environment increase with work experience.

Erroneous stereotype #3: *Millennials are the entitled generation.*

Counter to the stereotype that millennials are needier of their managers and have a higher sense of entitlement, millennials cited proportionally lower reasons for leaving in job characteristics and management behavior categories than other generations. In fact, millennials and GenXers are almost identical in the distribution of their reasons for leaving. This goes against the stereotypes that millennials are different from other groups in their attitudes and expectations. Their stage in life and career may have more to do with reasons for leaving than any sense of entitlement.[35]

Reducing turnover and increasing intent to stay require a strategy that accounts for multiple reasons, as different people appear to have different needs, preferences, and priorities across life stages.

> I am often invited to be a guest speaker on the topics of engagement and retention. Inevitably, the topic of millennials is brought up. While prior generations seem to have always found fault with younger ones, millennials seem to be taking much more than any deserved criticism.

Conference participants inevitably describe their younger employees as pampered, over-parented, and entitled. Stereotypes are created to suggest that millennials are unmanageable, impatient, and addicted to cell phones. In some way, too, I am told they have depression, somehow caused by not getting enough 'likes' in social media. Am I exaggerating? If you don't believe it, just ask them. Watching the reaction of the millennials in the room (and knowing the data) tells everything one needs to know.

Millennials only want what most generations wanted when they were in their twenties and thirties—development and comfort that they are being prepared for the future. Today's difference is in the employment marketplace. As opportunities are available and employers continue to compete for talent, employment choices abound. Younger employees are not being silent about their options; many of them are quitting. Now employers have the choice to stay silent . . . or respond.

—Danny A. Nelms

The data just do not support a generally held belief that younger employees have different preferences, expectations, and intents in the workplace than do middle-age and older employees.

Erroneous stereotype #4: *Employees don't leave companies; employees leave supervisors.*

Research with over 240,000 former employees demonstrated that 63 percent rated their employer "very good" or "excellent," and 66 percent of employees rated their supervisor "good" or "excellent."[36]

Companies who intervene on turnover and intent to stay by only assuming supervisors and managers require training may be intervening in the wrong place.

As the economy has shifted to an employee-in-control marketplace, we are seeing that workers are staying or leaving for preventable reasons, such as career development. Companies who require engagement and retention improvement need to diagnose and change the aspects of the workplace that reinforce employees to stay or cause them to leave, rather than assigning erroneous reasons to populations or citing wrong or incomplete data (e.g., "Millennials only stay for a short time anyway because they have no loyalty," or "The average person changes careers six or seven or nine times in his or her lifetime."). Companies can avoid the errors inherent in popular and common stereotypes by instead looking into and considering the preferences, expectations, and intents of their unique workforce.

IGNORING TROUBLED AND TROUBLING MANAGER BEHAVIORS

Management behavior is one of the more controllable categories of reasons why employees quit or intend to quit. Providing good managers and supervisors is both a responsibility and an opportunity for employers.

Some of today's managers have work problems. Emotional reactions, poor decision-making, bad supervisory behavior, inferior communication skills, and strained relationships—these work problems have a devastating effect on job performance, the overall workplace, and the people under one's supervision. A troubled or troubling manager presents difficulties for the organization, coworkers, supervisors, and employees, and can negatively affect retention, morale, productivity, and engagement. Compromising and inappropriate behaviors additionally place a company at risk for willful negligence, negligent hiring, and negligent retention.

Looking at the trend since 2010, employees are increasingly leaving organizations due to manager behavior. In 2017 and again in 2018, management behavior accounted for 11 percent of the reasons why employees left their organizations. Unprofessionalism in management behavior was a frequently occurring reason. Some examples include general management behavior (e.g., "I left because I had a [manager] that was terrible to work for."); lack of professionalism (e.g., "[My boss] shows a lot of favoritism to her friends at work."); failing to support employees (e.g., "My coworkers and I were not getting along well. I did not feel my manager was handling it properly."); and poor communication. Following are some qualitative responses from employees who quit, citing management behavior as the most important reason for their departure.

- "I left because of the leadership."

- "I did not think I had great support from leadership. My manager kept telling me I was doing a bad job and that I was not doing what I should be doing. Yet she would not tell me what I needed to do to improve."

- "I left because I had a director who was terrible to work for. They created a hostile work environment. She would constantly harass employees after work hours and weekends by calling us all the time about our work."

- "My direct supervisor, Jane Doe, was newly promoted, and she did not give good feedback. She did not care about anything but meeting numbers. That brought down morale."

- "I left there because I felt the management was out of touch with the staff. I felt management did not care and they did not have the employees' best interest at heart."

- "It was like pure chaos all the time. Management did not get along. There is no structure at all. One manager would say one thing and the other one would say something else."

- "I am actually bummed that I had to. I enjoyed my position; I was excited about the role and was getting good at it. But I did not fit in well with my manager, John Doe, and his management approach. John was just from the start, a micromanager . . ."

- "I was unsatisfied with the environment. My coworkers and I were not getting along well. I did not feel my manager was handling it properly."

- "John Doe, my supervisor, was a poor communicator. He could do a better job at trying to keep a level head in stressful situations."

- "I found a new position elsewhere. I feel that there is better management at my new position. There is transparency and a transformational leadership style. They value feedback from their front-line employees."

- "Severe lack of transparency with leadership. During my tenure we had a change, roughly two years ago, of our chief, and this has been extremely detrimental to the sense of teamwork and vision building in the department . . ."

- "I was being harassed by one of the supervisors within the company."

- "John Doe created a hostile work environment. He trained by yelling and belittling the crew. It has been going on for six years, so between 2011 and . . . now, in July 2017. It is in Engineering. This was in [Anytown, Anystate], at the main campus . . ."

- "A manager, Jane Doe, is very abusive and bullies the employees. She will talk down to all of us and attempt to make us feel lower than her. She shows a lot of favoritism to her friends at work. She handpicks people for her team, so they will protect her."

- "I was in a situation where I needed help, and I was not getting help from management. I made a decision to leave."

- "My supervisor never stood up for her team."

- "There is not enough supervision or coaching. If I had a question about documentation, I would ask my coworkers, but everyone [was] busy. I felt isolated."

- "I left because I did not think that upper management respected me and the other nurses as being professionals. They asked us for ideas, but they did not implement any ideas, or ever come back to us with reasons why they could or would not implement those . . ."

Intervening with managers around specific behaviors and expecting them to increase employees' ratings of their supervisory and management skills from "very good" to "excellent" will double the odds that the employee will stay with the company for a long time.

Assessing and taking action on troubled or troubling manager behavior is a win for an organization. Properly handled, an organization can accomplish the following:

- Return a valuable employee, who otherwise may have been lost or may have continued in a nonproductive manner, to productive status.

- Reassure employees that management is responsive to individual employee concerns.

- Avoid unnecessary terminations and potential lawsuits, costs, problems, and conflicts that may arise.

- Identify organizational, situational, and managerial irregularities that may contribute to compromised performance.

- Establish a system to deal effectively with performance problems as a permanent feature of the management function.

- Establish a system for companies to take time to look at themselves, to evaluate their problems, and to review their relationships.

An organization starves itself into nonexistence when it fails to ask, listen, and communicate to the sustaining source of productivity: the workforce.

THINKING ENGAGEMENT AND RETENTION IS A HUMAN RESOURCE DEPARTMENT RESPONSIBILITY

Attraction, recruitment, engagement, and retention. We get it. It sounds like they go together. They don't. Typically imbedded as an HR department responsibility is the requirement to support the organization by making sure there are enough proficient and engaged people to do the work that needs to be done. HR departments define and classify jobs, nurture a pipeline of applicants, interview for fit, and either hire or recommend and refer to business-unit decision makers. These days, however, for some misguided reason, HR departments have assumed or been assigned additional responsibility for engagement and retention. This is a mistake.

Line and operational managers must own retention and engagement. Organizations must hold direct supervisors accountable, including for creating and managing the organizational conditions aligned with employee preferences, expectations, and intents.

Holding operational managers accountable for retention will change manager behavior and increase retention.

STOP AND THINK

At Renal Advantage, Dean Weiland, COO, and Dr. Linda Meador, CHRO, attributed retention success to the fact that regional managers were held accountable for retention. Bonuses throughout were specifically tied to increased "excellent" ratings and reductions in turnover.

If your managers and supervisors were held accountable for engagement and retention, how might that change their behavior toward employees?

What would managers and supervisors do differently?

What might they stop doing?

What might they start doing?

PREOCCUPATION WITH DATA—*ONLY*

A recent "Quotable Quote" in the local business journal read: "The greatest asset in healthcare is data." Really? What about flu vaccines, antibiotics, MRIs, surgeons, nurses, pharmacists, informed patients? What about health itself? This is brought up because sometimes it appears that HR and other management professionals believe that employee-engagement-survey data is a "greatest asset." The survey or data reports alone, in many cases, seems to be the product, an accomplishment. This it is not.

Some organizations have confused survey activity and data reports with accomplishment. Improved engagement, increased productivity, increased retention, increased contribution, and increased growth, among other things, are possible accomplishments. Data is not the greatest asset. Effecting evidence-based accomplishment is the asset.

"No research without action, no action without research."
—Kurt Lewin

There is more to be done. It is necessary for HR and leadership to move beyond data gathering and repeated re-review (i.e., reworking, relooking, and revising data reports; changing bar charts to pie charts and pie charts to bar charts; changing the colors and/or the pagination, and then making another slide for yet another PowerPoint presentation). Data needs to be moved from problem diagnosis to action and ongoing evaluation. Leadership must move beyond data gathering and reporting behaviors and move into actual accomplishment.

Don't confuse behavior with accomplishment.

RECRUITING WRONGLY

A story is told of a guy who was interviewing for a new job. He was met at the elevator by the HR director. The director took him up to the top floor and showed him the view of the mountains and the snow-covered peaks. He walked him into the executive dining room, where the waiter brought him cappuccino, fresh fruit, and shortbread. The day continued with collegial introductions and conversation and tours of the gym, sauna, and windowed offices. The day ended with the job offer, job acceptance, and planned start date. All was good.

When the new employee arrived on the agreed-upon day and time, he was met by security, wanded, fingerprinted, photographed, escorted to the elevator, and introduced to the third subbasement. On his way to his dark, damp, newly assigned workspace, he saw that he could purchase a sandwich and a cup of coffee from the vending machine. With promises that someone would be in shortly to introduce him to his assignments, he waited in his empty cubicle through lunchtime.

Early afternoon had him calling up to HR and inquiring about the prehire promise, the absent views, the vending machines, and the lack of direction.

He was told, "Well, that was all true when we were recruiting you; now you are ours."

The typical vacancy today costs about $22,000 per position over the average period of forty-four days.[37] Many companies ignore these costs while continuing to make significant and manageable errors with both employees who choose to leave and those who are trying to join. Work Institute Recruitment Analysis Studies have identified the following mistakes:

- Top applicants vanish during the hiring decision-making process. Companies promise to get back to people by a certain time, but rarely do. Applicants go elsewhere.

- Companies are taking too long to decide. Applicants go elsewhere.

- Hires result in unsatisfactory results. Interview skills development; reference checking; job previews; and properly selected, scored, and interpreted personality, skills-motivation, interest, and work-value assessments can increase hiring success.

- Top employees depart within a few months. Companies need to be more transparent with job previews and expectations.

- Managers struggle to identify critical aspects of the best candidate. Sometimes, given a history of hiring failures, managers are reluctant to make the decision.

- Candidates are exposed to continuous rounds of interviews that confuse assessing with selling. Candidates go elsewhere.

Perhaps the greatest mistake is made by organizations that confuse recruiting with technology. Neither recruiting nor hiring is an electronic application. Hiring is about initiating an employment relationship. Recruiting software may ease administrative tasks by checking to see that the correct search words are in the electronic résumé, or may send programmed rejection letters, but that is not recruiting. Companies are losing potential and necessary employees, with the erroneous belief that the newest best-in-breed technology will do the job.

Don't automate stupid.

Human resources directors, as owners of recruitment, do not typically have feedback channels in place to effectively capture and accurately understand the candidate recruitment experience. In today's competitive employee-attraction environment, it is necessary for employers to understand why candidates are or are not accepting offers and what can improve hiring ratios. Employers can improve recruitment if they understand, manage, and continuously evaluate recruitment effectiveness. Done properly, managers can

- understand perceived strengths and weaknesses of the recruitment process and requirements for improvement;

- understand the real reasons why candidates accept or decline offers and what needs to be done to increase accepts, as well as the reasons why applicants chose an alternate employer;

- explore the likelihood a candidate would reconsider a future role with your organization;

- understand line-manager perspectives on new employee quality of hire; and

- obtain insight around employee performance, satisfaction with time to productivity, and employee fit within the organization.

HIRING POORLY

Employees leave for preventable reasons within the first year. This is a major cost to companies. Realistic job previews, illustrating the actual expectations of the manager and requirements of the job, must be thoroughly explained and sometimes demonstrated prior to hire. It may require additional time, but in the long run it will pay off with improved retention. Five of the top ten reasons (three of the top five) are preventable and could be circumvented by better prehire assessments, job previews, and onboarding, including career development.

As employer-specific data supports it, employers would do well to enroll new employees in a career management plan from day one. Early enrollment reinforces an employer's commitment to the employee.

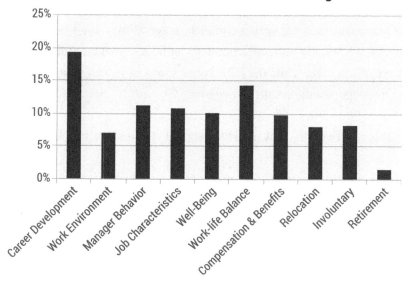

First Year Turnover Reasons for Leaving

"As to methods there may be a million and then some, but principles are few. The [person] who grasps principles can successfully select [their] own methods. The [person] who tries methods, ignoring principles, is sure to have trouble." [amended]
—Ralph Waldo Emerson

NOT RETHINKING YOUR METHODS

Today we are deluged with results from the latest polls. One poll says Facebook will increase your self-esteem, while the other poll says it causes alienation and depression. Global warming is real in one study and a made-up creation in the next. According to Bureau X, eggs, coffee, and wine are good for you, but a study from another authority says they are not. The pharmaceutical company reports the drug is a lifesaver while the class action study says it will cost you a liver. Election polling predicted Hillary as the shoo-in for president in 2016. Polls on gun laws report Americans simultaneously want stricter and less strict regulations. In yesterday's newspaper poll, Democrats said yes and Republicans said no, with a complete reversal in today's newspaper poll. CNN's study said with complete confidence that the study results were affirmative, while the FOX News study, also with complete certainty, reported the results as negative.

It is trustworthy that poorly designed studies can't be trusted.

These are serious times for our companies. The economy is offering significant opportunity for company growth, but turnover is at an all-time high, engagement is stagnant or diminishing, and the number of people available to work is limited.

Many vendors will recommend a traditional ratings-based engagement or satisfaction survey to diagnose and act on the reasons for retention, turnover, and so-labeled disengagement, but this may not work in an employee-in-control market. Given today's employees' market, there are serious flaws with traditional approaches that will lead to wasted expense, investments in the wrong workplace changes, or no action at all. With all the conflicting "expert" information, to have confidence, employers need to be better consumers of research. Following are a few recommendations regarding

- selection of a research provider,

- questions,

- response rate and single subjects,

- scoring, and

- action.

SELECTION OF A RESEARCH PROVIDER

Companies sometimes err in hiring solution providers to conduct employee research. If the employer hires a benefits company to do the employee survey, they will be changing the benefits program. If the employer hires a compensation company, the compensation programs will be revised, and wage inflation is sure to follow. The leadership development group tells you all problems are solved through their proprietary-management and supervisory-development programs and their consultants' long-term coaching process. And on it goes. Sometimes companies select a survey firm that has already determined what they're going to sell, regardless of actual retention and engagement requirements.

When selecting an employee survey provider, make sure recommended questions are not biased toward the vendor's off-the-rack solutions (e.g., "How do you rate compensation?" "How do you rate benefits?" "How do you rate your supervisor?"). Be cautious about accepting recommendations or implementing solutions that just happen to be directed toward the provider's primary business.

QUESTIONS

Questions asked have a major impact on the utility of the answers obtained. As previously discussed in chapter one, the predetermined, biased themes of typical and popular models for measuring employee engagement and retention are self-limiting.

In the broadest sense, there are two basic types of questions: (a) open-ended questions and (b) closed-ended questions. Open-ended (qualitative) questions have the advantage of eliciting issues that are most salient to the respondent. Open-ended questions identify action priorities. Closed-ended questions take many forms. The most common types are ratings (e.g., excellent, very good, good, fair, poor); agreement (e.g., strongly agree, agree, disagree, strongly disagree, and yes/no/maybe); importance (e.g., very important, important, somewhat important, not important); and frequency (e.g., often, sometimes, seldom, never). These types of questions present specific statements, usually predetermined by the survey publisher or believed important by an organization. With closed-ended questions, respondents react to what the organization thinks the issues are, rather than allowing the respondent to identify and rate the most salient issues to them. It is recommended that employers combine open-ended questions with closed-ended questions in order to obtain the most actionable intelligence possible.

Why do you plan on staying for a long time? What else, what else, what else? Of these reasons what is the most important?

Given increasing market pressures for employers to attract, engage, and retain talent, understanding why employees leave and which employees are at risk of leaving in the short term becomes important. Rather than depend on traditional and predefined question survey methods, open-ended questions increase the predictive power to identify at-risk employees and identify the causative conditions. Alongside other benefits, a probing interview approach brings more comprehensive data, stronger causal understanding, and employee satisfaction that his or her voice is truly heard. Companies need to incorporate such interview practices and methodologies into employee research efforts to effect the greatest impact on retention and engagement.[38]

Approaching employee impressions from an open-ended method

allows the employee to voice real workplace observations and concerns, without limiting the employee's responses. Identifying the most important workplace strengths (drivers) and weaknesses (restraints) illuminates areas necessary for improvement.

Think about it this way: instead of asking twenty-five additional, different rating questions about the employees' issues, just ask them why. It is the difference between asking someone, "Would you like to travel to Hawaii or Colorado for vacation?" versus asking, "If you could travel anywhere in the world, where would you want to go, and why?"

STOP AND THINK

How about you? When do you plan to look for a new job? In the next thirty days, in the next ninety days, six months, two years, or not for a long time?

What would need to be different to increase your length of stay with your current employer?

What else? What else?

Of those reasons, which is the most important?

RESPONSE RATE AND SINGLE SUBJECTS

Adjusted response rates of around 50 percent or higher are essential to trust that the conclusions obtained from survey data are representative of the fuller population. If managers select enterprise-wide priorities for improvement based on data obtained with a less than 50 percent response rate, they are at risk of erroneous conclusions over half the time.[39]

Regardless of response rate and opportunity to generalize results and subsequent action to all employees, there is often an equally important reason to understand the preferences, expectations, and intents of individuals and smaller groups. Individual behavioral intent implies the motivation to act on a planned behavior. As you learn of reasons why individuals or smaller groups intend to stay or leave, the opportunity to intervene, regardless of generalizability to the full population, is required.

Upon entering the front doors of the Work Institute, one is greeted with a sign that says, "Build a better workplace, one employee at a time." While understanding and generalizing survey data to larger populations can yield important insights, companies must not fail to recognize that organizations are made up of individuals.

Consider the accounting department with five employees:

- The analyst needs scheduling flexibility to transport his kids to school and attend the school play.

- The new CPA wants a clear career path to increase confidence that she can grow with the company.

- The seasoned controller is offended by the micromanagement behaviors of the CFO and wants a bit more autonomy to make decisions.

- The accounts payable clerk simply wants job stability and recognition for good work.

- Another accountant is nearing retirement and is worried about his health and his ability to financially transition out of full-time work.

Each person has unique circumstances. Intervening solely on company reasons may not respond to individual or role requirements.

SCORING

Research supports using the five-point scale, which in general has good reliability and validity.[40] In a test between four- and five-point scales, the five-point scale had less missing data, higher internal consistency, and smaller floor and ceiling effects.[41] Conversely, with agree/disagree rating scales, the most valid and reliable data has been produced with five-point scales rather than seven- or eleven-point scales.[42]

One of the scoring mistakes companies often make with rating scales is grouping scores for reporting. It is not unusual for a company to group "fair," "good," "very good," and "excellent" and report the cumulative score as favorable. Consider the following score distribution example:

Excellent (5)	Very Good (4)	Good (3)	Fair (2)	Poor (1)
n=160	n=100	n=500	n=100	n=140
16%	10%	50%	10%	14%

Based on the above responses, some companies would report 86 percent of the employees as "favorable" and 14 percent as "unfavorable," because they combined results from employees who provided ratings of 5 (16 percent), 4 (10 percent), 3 (50 percent), and 2 (10 percent) and coded them as favorable, with 1 (14 percent) being the only unfavorable. Perhaps a more conservative company may report a "favorable" score of 76 percent and an "unfavorable" of 14 percent by adding the percentages of 5s, 4s, and 3s for favorable, and 1 (14 percent) as unfavorable. Regardless, this is a mistake.

A net excellence score (NES) is the recommended scoring procedure as it is statistically sound and practical to use for recommendations. Individuals who give an "excellent" rating are categorized as positives; those who give a "very good" or "good" rating are categorized as neutrals. Those who give a "fair" or "poor" rating are categorized as negatives. This scoring procedure has the advantage of reporting the proportion of employees with strong positive perceptions, while also considering employees who have strong negative perceptions.[43] The NES scoring scale has a significant relationship with intent to stay and is easy for organizations to understand and explain to employees.

Addressing the above posted scores then offers a more realistic picture. Favorables are now 16 percent, and unfavorables are 24 percent. This company's "low-hanging fruit" opportunity is to reduce the unfavorables and increase the favorables.

ACTION

To improve employee attraction and retention, a company must act on company specific requirements. While it is enticing to hear about a new approach or solution that has been successful elsewhere, employers must align actions to areas evidenced by company-unique data.

ASSUMING COLLEGE PREPARES STUDENTS FOR WORK

A compelling issue over the next several years is the absence of employees ready to assume the requirements of the workplace. There is limited employee availability and a critical skills and knowledge crisis.

Some of the greatest accomplishments of humankind, from knowledge creation to discoveries in health, engineering, technology, and service, came out of the university. Employers were confident in the learning and training provided, and increasingly "degree required" was a standard tag on job postings. Sometimes the employer believed degreed employees were needed for the work to done. Arguably, it may also have been true that, in a different economy, requiring a degree helped eliminate an abundance of applicants. Something changed.

Some facts:

- Fifty-five percent of high school students do not believe they're ready for college or work.[44]

- Forty-five percent of students do not demonstrate significant improvement in critical thinking and analytical reasoning during the first two years of college.[45]

- Among young high school graduates, about 23 percent fail to achieve the qualifying score to join the US Army. "Just as secondary schools are failing to prepare many students for college and civilian careers, so too are they failing to prepare young men and women—particularly young people of color—for military service. For these young Americans, a high school diploma does not qualify them to 'be all that you can be.'"[46]

- According to the Pentagon, of the 34 million seventeen- to twenty-four-year-olds in the US, 71 percent would not qualify for military service because of health, physical appearance, or educational background.[47]

- Today's dropouts spend at least nine years in school; over half are functionally illiterate and innumerate.[48]

- The American Revolution Center tested one thousand adult Americans' knowledge of the American Revolution, and only 17 percent passed.[49]

- The Intercollegiate Studies Institute tested over twenty-five hundred adult Americans' knowledge of American government and American history, and 71 percent failed.[50]

- Out of students who started four-year public colleges in 2005, 32 percent finished on time and 56 percent finished in six years.[51]

- The overall graduation rate for graduate and professional school is 50 percent.[52]

- Despite a significant increase in funding for education, there were no statistically significant differences in the average prose and document literacy (the skills to search, comprehend, and use information) of the adult population of the US from 1992 to 2003. Quantitative literacy (skills needed to identify and perform computations using numbers) increased slightly.[53]

- Employers give graduates low marks for workforce preparedness.[54] If the earnings premium for high school and college graduates is 70 percent and 30 percent respectively, and graduates do not have the skills and knowledge necessary to do the job, why are employers paying a premium?

Perhaps driven by a sense that current curricula and teaching methods are failing to prepare students for the work that needs to be done, discovery and learning that once came out of college is increasingly delivered by employers. As the academy is not preparing a ready workforce, companies are building learning organizations to provide necessary training, including remediation in reading, writing, arithmetic, and social skills. Private enterprise, rather than the university, is building competency certification programs wherein learners demonstrate mastery of specific skills and knowledge.

It may be time to reevaluate the need for everyone to pursue a higher degree. Companies are bearing the expense to train a ready workforce, and schools are not designing curricula based on economic and community development requirements. Concurrently, it may be time for employers to help the high schools and community colleges redesign curricula and verify it supports workplace requirements.

STOP AND THINK

Does that job description you are writing really require a degree? Why?

"Though silence is not necessarily an admission, it is not a denial, either."
—Marcus Tullius Cicero

OVERLOOKING UNETHICAL, FRAUDULENT, AND BEHAVIORAL ISSUES

Employees are rarely surprised upon hearing of an incident of unethical, fraudulent, or criminal behavior and often respond with "All the signs were there." If organizational members see all the signs, why the reluctance to report and intervene?

Workplace misconduct is not restricted to overt acts. It includes workers' acting out and aggressively confronting supervisors, supervisees, and colleagues, and it includes more subtle behaviors that compromise people, productivity, and organizations. In 2017, the following made headlines:

- Sexual harassment and sexual harassment allegations plagued multiple companies, including headline-making claims at 21st Century Fox, NPR, the US Congress, Bank of America, and Fox News.

- A credit-reporting company, with previous knowledge about system flaws, allowed the personal information on 145 million people (about half the US population) to be hacked. In 2019, this company was fined $700,000,000.

- A steel company falsified information on items sold to airline and auto companies.

- International automakers were forced to recall 1.6 million vehicles, reporting they allowed unqualified inspectors to conduct final inspections on vehicles.

- A top-10 US bank charged up to 570,000 consumers for auto insurance they did not need. The same bank revealed it created up to 3.5 million accounts without customer permission.

- A cell phone company slowed phones to compensate for decaying batteries.

- A hospital management and ownership company provided kickbacks to physician groups for patient referrals.

- OSHA issued fines for safety violations that employees were aware of but either failed to report or ignored in their reporting.

The list goes on, but it doesn't have to. School shootings, sexual abuse in university locker rooms, and bullying can all be avoided if information is shared and acted upon.

STOP AND THINK

Are you aware of any harmful, unethical, illegal, or financial impropriety within your organization?

The percentage of employees reporting awareness of unethical, illegal, or fraudulent behavior at their former place of employment reached 6.1 percent in 2017, a steady increase from just 1.0 percent in 2010. As the market emerged from the recession, workers increasingly left employers where perceived misconduct was present.

As long as workplace misconduct is tolerated, this rise is likely to continue.

Fraud, abuse, ethics and financial violations, kickbacks, sexual harassment, weapons, drug use, threats, insurance and Medicaid fraud, discrimination, favoritism, theft, and bullying are just some of the concerns voiced by former employees—who waited until they left to report.

Employers may never know if there are more actual incidents of workplace misconduct than in prior years, or if notable social movements (#metoo, #neveragain) simply led workers to report incidents at a greater rate than in prior years. What is known, as market conditions remain strong and job opportunities continue to increase, is that workers no longer need to tolerate unacceptable behavior, as employees can choose to go elsewhere.

Increasingly, it is necessary for organizations to provide employees with ongoing avenues to report misconduct. Rather than depend on passive and rarely utilized 1-800 lines, companies alternatively can proactively and routinely solicit and document awareness (and the absence) of harmful, illegal, unethical, and noncompliant behavior. To minimize harm, employers can create a positive work environment, create ways for all employees to bring forward concerns about questionable behaviors, and act on employee input.

Employers must solicit and act on reports of misbehavior or read about it in the headlines.

IGNORING CAREER DEVELOPMENT

Akiva, the rabbi, had been in the village to gather some supplies. Later in the evening while mindlessly walking back to his cottage, he took the wrong path. Suddenly, a loud voice came through the darkness, reclaiming his attention: "Who are you, and why are you here?"

Shocked, Akiva realized he had wandered mistakenly to the gates of the Roman garrison. Regaining his senses and realizing the voice had come from a Roman sentry, he answered the young sentry's inquiry with another question. "How much do they pay you to stand guard and ask that question to all who approach?" The sentry, seeing that this was a rabbi and not an intruder, answered, "Five drachmas a week, Rabbi."

The rabbi said, "Young man, I will double your pay if you come to my house and ask me, each day, who are you and why are you here?"

—Anonymous

As one core reason that people stay or quit, career development may be a valuable consideration for both the employer and the employee. Organizational competitiveness requires that companies have the skilled people to do the work when it needs to get done. Companies cannot stay competitive if they are constantly losing their best people. The 2017, 2018, and 2019 Work Institute Retention Reports make it quite clear: employees in general are yelling loudly that they left or intend to leave either because the tasks companies promised them never appeared, tasks they didn't anticipate ended up on their plate, promotional opportunities were given to less-productive employees with longer tenure or to new hires from outside, or employees don't have the confidence that they are being prepared or being given the opportunity to do the work employers will need in the near future.

On the rise for the last seven years, career development is the most popular category of reasons employees quit. Career development includes the following:

- **Type of work:** Employee expectations may not have matched with the type of work actually involved, where perhaps the educational system or hiring processes did not provide a realistic view of the job. For example, "I started to realize that hospital nursing was not for me. The work setting was really lonely since I worked in the ICU department." Perhaps knowing this could have helped the employee find opportunity in a more team-based department and helped the employer hold on to a skilled nurse. By some estimates, losing an ICU nurse could cost more than $125,000.

- **Growth and development:** Employees often left because they wanted to learn, grow, and be challenged in their work, and another employer offered better opportunities to do just that (e.g., "I left to take a position elsewhere that offered me more growth opportunities."). Often growth opportunity is available to an employee; they just don't know it. Having an active and advertised career counselor available to employees will help with their self-awareness and career opportunity, and help employers retain skilled and growth-oriented employees.

- **School:** Some employees may have only planned to work for a set period before returning to school, while for others work experiences caused them to rethink their career path and invest in further education. Regardless, employee departure creates costs, and the company misses an opportunity to retain an employee (e.g., "I started back to school and needed the time for my studies.").

- **Promotion:** Often employees had applied for promotions at their previous employer unsuccessfully before making the decision to leave (e.g., "I left for a supervisory position with another company that offered advancement."). It is often the case that high-achieving employees leave because they see underperforming but longer-tenured employees get the promotion, or they are restricted from promotion by policy (e.g., "An employee must be in a role for two years before being considered for another position."). Change the policy or lose the high-achieving employee.

"Less than 20 percent are very satisfied with their career development opportunities. . . . However, those who were very satisfied with their career development opportunities were more likely to plan to remain with their current employer."
—Career Agility and Engagement Research[55]

Companies, if their data supports the career development requirement, are advised to implement a career development strategy to support career growth, improve retention, and create the conditions necessary for individual motivation and productivity. Self-awareness, choice, planning, and action are critical to a career management program. Such programs should optimally include opportunities for employees (and the organization) to

- learn about employee vocational self-concept, including who the employee is, where and how the employee does his or her best work, and with whom the employee does the best work. This includes assessments in the areas of occupational personality, values, skill motivation, and interests;

- identify and learn about occupational alternatives at the company;

- understand the process, including preparation and skill development requirements, for selected alternatives;

- implement vocational choice. Customized career plans can be developed to include project work, stretch assignments, mentors, or temporary changing of roles; and

- continue to manage career by constantly asking and answering the questions, Who are you, and where are you going?

Employees increasingly are more aware of the need to take control of their career—a control they can manage with their current employer or elsewhere.

STOP AND THINK

Who are you, and why are you here?

FOUR

Costing Human Behavior

I sit in two chairs. On one hand I am a workplace behavior scientist; I am also the CEO of the Work Institute. In these roles, I am comforted by the fact that human behavior in the workplace is predictable and, if one asks and truly listens, relatively simple to understand. I am concurrently burdened that companies struggle with productivity improvements. I believe they make it too complicated. In this economy, which is dependent on human behavior, productivity improvements and profits increase with improved employee and customer relationships.
—Thomas F. Mahan

Reducing human capital scrap and waste improves profits.

As an organization, Renal Advantage, an outpatient dialysis services company with centers in eighteen states, set an objective to have the total "intent to leave within one year" at less than 15 percent. The human resources department, in close partnership with operational managers, served as the driver of this process. With the support of the executive leadership team, employees worked with the Work Institute to develop the questionnaire. To maximize RAI's ability to set targets and measure the progress toward their goals, a five-point-rating-scale question design (excellent, very good, good, fair, and poor) was used. Follow-up questions, such as "Why?" and "What would it take to get an 'excellent' rating?" allowed for the gathering of more detailed information. The qualitative data provided the organization with actionable data that drove evidence-based decisions to earn employees' highest endorsement.

The Work Institute surveyed the entire workforce to gather baseline data, and goals were set based on the initial results. Six months later, the Work Institute interviewed 50 percent of the workforce to begin the biannual surveys. Once the two data points had been collected and analyzed, Dr. Linda Meador, Vice President of Human Resources, and Christie Carlisle, Director of Human Resources, traveled to each RAI region to equip supervisors with the tools and techniques needed to build and execute action plans.

By the end of the year, RAI evaluated all interventions and celebrated the successes of their evidence-based action-planning initiatives, using data obtained from the employee surveys.

Following internal adjustments, employee pulse surveys indicated that satisfaction with RAI drastically increased. The number of employees who rated their employer as "excellent" increased by 22 percent; the number of employees who rated their supervisors as "excellent" improved by 10 percent; and the number of employees with an intent to leave within the first year at RAI decreased from 22 percent to 16 percent. Most importantly, turnover dropped from 29 percent to 7 percent.

Together, quantitative and qualitative measures inform.

Employers must trust that employees know and can inform what needs to happen to create better relationships. Organizational behavior management (OBM) research continues to illustrate the value of employee participation.[56] Rather than merely collecting data *about* people, employers can learn *from* people. Employees will report what practices are needed in their organization—when, where, and with whom.

Ask, hear, communicate. Thank employees for their input. Do something to effect necessary changes. As beneficial to the employee and the organization, continuously evaluate additional changes required by again asking, hearing, acknowledging, and thanking employees for input. Then repeat.

PRODUCTIVITY

Traditionally defined, *productivity* is a measure calculated by looking at the ratio of revenue from goods, relative to the costs of labor, materials, and overhead to directly produce those goods. Productivity is a measure of economic efficiency, and it is how organizational dollars are converted into profit.

- Productivity improves when organizational dollars produce more profit with the same or less expense.

- Productivity worsens when organizational dollars produce less profit with more expense.

Historically, productivity has been represented in the following formula:

$$Manufacturing\ Productivity = \frac{revenue\ from\ goods}{cost\ of\ labor,\ materials,\ and\ overhead\ (COG)}$$

This equation for productivity fit well in agricultural and manufacturing economies. It was simple. Productivity was the sales income divided by the costs of the workers necessary to manipulate the materials into sellable and deliverable product and the raw materials and overhead necessary to produce the products.

The long and substantial growth and profitability in manufacturing during the 1950s and 1960s boosted the US economy. Following WWII, as Europe and Japan lost manufacturing due to wartime destruction and pre- and post-war trade agreements, the US was producing product for the world and the US economy was booming. Most attention went to growth and just keeping up with demand, and compromised attention was given to manufacturing improvements and product quality. Manufacturing was seduced into complacency, just keeping up with the norms. Mediocrity was evidenced by unkempt production areas, poorly maintained equipment, inaccurate inventory counts, excessive scrap, accidents, and subpar quality. (A comparison might be made between yesterday's poorly maintained equipment, inaccurate inventory counts, excessive scrap, accidents, and subpar quality and today's relationship with employees.)

Productivity levels were fine, or so everyone thought. However, driven by less severe trade agreements, quality problems, and the post-war rebuild of Japanese manufacturing, American consumers traded in Fords and Chevys for Datsuns, Hondas, and Toyotas. Japanese manufacturers produced lower-cost and higher-quality products, and US manufacturers were losing sales in everything from automobiles to televisions and toasters. The Japanese changed business and manufacturing practices worldwide.

In time, US manufacturers acknowledged their product and quality inefficiencies and they responded. In 1977, just-in-time production (JIT) was introduced to guide manufacturing operations. Competition was severe, and if the US wanted to acquire and keep market share, additional changes were required. Process improvement was initiated, followed by supply chain management. The US was making major strides in productivity and quality improvement.

As a continuous improvement strategy, US companies also started to do a better job of monitoring and managing manufacturing costs. Organizations reduced scrap and waste, cleaned up the floors, instituted maintenance schedules, and attended to safety concerns. Motorola, in its day, tracked labor and part manufacturing costs out four decimal places. Nothing happened on the production floor that wasn't routinely measured and cost accounted.

However:

Sales, general, and administrative (SG&A) costs were not managed in any detail. If spending was within budget and headcount objectives were met, free reign was given to department managers. Continuing today, albeit in a different area, companies are still not managing SG&A expenses. The result is widespread waste and diminished profit.

The world has changed and work has changed. Rarely today is an employee bending steel; machines do it. Assembly lines are increasingly staffed by robots, hamburgers are flipped by mechanical arms, software is drafting our correspondence, our phones track movement and traffic patterns, coffee is prepared by robots, and drones are security officers.

Worker demand and skills today are different than yesterday, and human behavior increasingly is the competitive advantage. Organizations need to have relationships with the right people, with the right skills, at the right time.

As scrap and waste was once accepted as the cost of doing business, today's scrap and waste resides in cost per hire, recruitment costs, engagement/satisfaction/commitment costs, and turnover costs. Companies can and must avoid accepting losses in these areas as merely "the cost of doing business." Employee turnover, for example, costs companies hundreds of billions of dollars every year.

The opportunity for companies to reduce costs is significant. A "low-hanging fruit" today is in the employment relationship arena, including reducing turnover, improving engagement, and eliminating misbehavior. Just because these costs are budgeted does not justify them as acceptable. Too often, managers excuse these losses as a "cost of doing business." It is time to add all SG&A expenses to the denominator of the productivity equation.

$$\textit{Human Capital Productivity} = \frac{\textit{revenue from goods and services}}{\textit{cost of labor, SG\&A, materials, and overhead}}$$

Clever people make changes as necessary, when compelled. In the manufacturing economy, companies recognized growth and profitability required changes in supply, quality, delivery processes, and waste reduction. In this current, increasingly employee-dependent economy, changes are necessary in employee attraction, recruitment, performance, engagement, and retention. It is also time to make changes in the way we measure and manage human capital.

Again, the low-hanging fruit to decreasing costs in manufacturing required reducing material costs due to error and material waste. Companies must look at their opportunities to reduce human capital costs. For example, if you reduced turnover and increased length-of-stay of necessary talent, how would that reduce human capital costs and increase productivity? Companies need to understand the costs of human behavior in the workplace, including the costs of recruitment, retention, and misbehavior.

Some companies (defensively) argue their turnover is lower than industry standards, or that their theft and shrinkage is less than the national norms. And, for some reason, that's okay with them. Complacency about turnover and other compromising behaviors is unacceptable and inexcusable, regardless of any standard.

Turnover, not unlike scrap, is costly and can be reduced. If people are leaving, or thinking about leaving, they are gone or not fully contributing. Similar to crawling over scrap or tripping on cable, employees who have left or are leaving are distracting and preventing others from achieving goals. How well would a national sports team or the local PTA succeed if players and volunteers were continuously leaving? Talent loss weighs down team spirit, as new players and volunteers must be continuously recruited, hired, trained, and assimilated into the existing culture. No Super Bowl for your team. No art and music for your kid's school.

Manufacturing calls scrap "wasted time and money." Companies need to understand that turnover and recruiting costs are unacceptable at any level and contribute to additional wasted time and money.

Consider this: For every three workers who leave a company, for the same expense there can be one additional full-time employee. How would that affect work-life balance and scheduling? Companies compete. If competition is efficiently managing turnover and you are not, you lose.

Consider a couple of examples of how to look at increasing human capital productivity: (1) the company can sell the same but reduce expenses, or (2) the company can sell more with the same expenses.

Consider #1: the company can sell the same but reduce expenses. Comparing the following income statements, employee expenses were reduced 15 percent through reducing turnover. So, the cost reduction of $1,062,000 correspondingly increases profits by the same amount, $1,062,000. Expense dollars, when reduced, go to the bottom line. In this case, productivity increased by reducing expenses.

Income Statement ($ in 000)	Income Statement No Turnover Reduction		Income Statement with 15% Reduction in Turnover (25% to 21.25%)	
Net Operating Revenue	$900,000		$900,000	
Cost of Goods Sold	630,000		630,000	
Gross Margin	270,000	30.0%	270,000	30.0%
Operating Expenses:				
Sales, Mkt., Gen'l Admin., etc.	150,000		150,000	
Human Capital Expenses:				
Compensation, Benefits,				
Workers' Comp, etc.	85,000		85,000	
SG&A-related Turnover Costs				
(25% Turnover)	7,083		6,021	
Total Expense	242,083		241,021	
Operating Income	$27,917	3.1%	$28,979	3.2%

Note: Turnover costs are reduced by $1,062,000, and profits are increased, dollar for dollar, by $1,062,000.

Now consider #2: the company can sell more with the same expenses. Comparing these income statements, employee expenses around turnover were not managed. So, to increase profit by the same $1,062,000, a sales increase of $3,540,000 is required.

To maintain the current level of efficiency, the company is required to cover every one dollar of expense with three dollars of revenue.

Income Statement ($ in 000)	Income Statement No Turnover Reduction		Income Statement with Sales Increase of $3,540,000	
Net Operating Revenue	$900,000		$903,540	
Cost of Goods Sold	630,000		632,478	
Gross Margin	270,000	30.0%	271,062	30.0%
Operating Expenses: Sales, Mkt., Gen'l Admin., etc.	150,000		150,000	
Human Capital Expenses: Compensation, Benefits, Workers' Comp, etc.	85,000		85,000	
SG&A-related Turnover Costs (25% Turnover)	7,083		7,083	
Total Expense	242,083		242,083	
Operating Income	$27,917	3.1%	$28,979	3.2%

Note: Without the 15 percent reduction in turnover costs, a sales increase of $3,540,000 is required.

STOP AND THINK
Now, if I'm the CEO, what is my expectation?

If I am the chief revenue officer, what is my expectation?

If I am the chief human resource officer, what is my expectation?

No matter the level of your company's turnover, retention can be improved and needs to be improved. As referenced in the above examples, for every turnover dollar spent, sales must cover it with three dollars in revenue.

Employers must understand the real reasons for engagement and retention and continuously monitor and improve the employment relationship. Human capital expenses are increasing. Turnover rates are up, filling positions is taking longer, benefits costs are skyrocketing, wage inflation is active or knocking at the door, and risk concerns continue to surface, costing money and derailing business objectives. Today's very manageable expenses include reductions in recruitment, hiring, temporary and staffing agencies, turnover, and behavior risk. As illustrated in the previous income statements, reducing manageable expenses is a way to increase productivity and profits.

An employer's inability to sell and deliver product or service drives customer loss and hurts the revenue line. Controllable expenses directly, dollar to dollar, reduce profit and threaten productivity. Managing controllable human-capital expenses reduces threats to production, sales, customer service, and retention.

People are a primary profit lever.

THE HUMAN CAPITAL AUDIT

Controllable human-capital expenses can be identified and quantified. Areas and information worth collecting, understanding, and managing, through a periodic human-capital audit, are listed below. As these costs and reasons are identified, employers can make ROI-based decisions, building a business case for financially advantageous solutions.

- Hiring costs, trends, and reasons
- Agency costs, trends, and reasons
- Employee turnover costs, trends, and reasons
- Unemployment insurance costs, trends, and reasons
- Behavior risk incidents, costs, trends, and reasons
- Workers' compensation costs, trends, and reasons

- Safety violation costs, trends, and reasons
- Employee relations costs, trends, and reasons
- Shrinkage/theft costs, trends, and reasons
- Absenteeism costs, trends, and reasons
- Learning and development costs, trends, and reasons

Audits can be completed in human-capital expense categories, and management objectives and plans can be built to reduce expenses. The following utilizes retention management—employee turnover costs, trends, and reasons—to illustrate a component of a human capital audit.

CALCULATE YOUR COST OF TURNOVER

Achieving business results in an intensely competitive employee marketplace demands that employers take proactive measures to predict and prevent turnover. Implemented effectively, human capital costing and employee-centric research provide the information needed to set correct objectives and accurately identify retention requirements, leading to direct cost savings.

Current trends show the competition for workers is escalating while the talent pool is shrinking. This intensifies an employee-in-control marketplace and places employers at risk of rising turnover costs among other things. As workers leave their jobs, employers incur direct turnover costs associated with separation, replacement, and training.[57] Organizations also incur indirect turnover costs through decreased organizational performance. The direct and indirect costs of turnover are estimated to be as much as one to two times the worker's salary, with an average of $4,129 in replacement costs alone.[58] Specific employee turnover costs include expenses incurred by employees' leaving (exit processing, separation pay, accrued vacation pay, benefits continuation, and unemployment tax and insurance); replacement costs (advertising, agency fees, overtime, referral bonuses, travel, relocation, recruiter costs/search fees, interviewing, drug tests, selection testing, reference checks); training costs; and vacancy costs (decreased performance, employee and customer reaction brought on by vacancy).

"Benchmark" data of turnover costs are all over the board. Various studies will suggest that an hourly employee turnover can cost anywhere from $4,129 to the equivalent of six months' salary. For a salaried employee, costs of turnover can range from $9,000 to upward of two times the annual salary. Specific critical employee turnover costs can be greater. For example, an absent ICU nurse costs patient beds' being filled. A key salesperson, a technical expert, or a key executive can cost even more.

Rather than depending on others' estimates, employers are encouraged to determine their own cost models and confirm agreement from finance, operations, and HR. As an actual cost per person is agreed upon, employers can accurately identify the actual value of an intervention to identify turnover reasons, intent-to-turnover reasons, stay reasons, and ROI-based interventions.

Using one-third of an employee's annual salary as an example and assuming an average salary of $45,000, one might estimate turnover cost as $15,000.

Est. Turnover Cost Percent of Salary	33%
Median US Worker Salary	$45,000
Average Cost of Turnover	$15,000

Calculating that out to the number of employees who left or intend to leave, one can calculate the organizational cost of turnover and turnover risk.

Number of Employees	2018 Turnover Rate %	2018 Turnover Number	2018 Turnover Cost
100	25%	25	$375,000
1,000	25%	250	$3,750,000
10,000	25%	2,500	$37,500,000
100,000	25%	25,000	$375,000,000

As an additional example, calculating the individual cost of turnover for a ten-dollar-per-hour employee at $5,000 yields the following:

Number of Employees	2018 Turnover Rate %	2018 Turnover Number	2018 Turnover Cost
100	25%	25	$125,000
1,000	25%	250	$1,250,000
10,000	25%	2,500	$12,500,000
100,000	25%	25,000	$125,000,000

Voluntary turnover cost US companies more than $600 billion in 2018, as one in four employees quit to take a different job. Should voluntary quit rates continue as projected, turnover costs will increase to nearly $680 billion in 2020, a 19 percent increase from 2017.

BUILD A BUSINESS CASE FOR RETENTION MANAGEMENT

Using the most conservative (direct cost) turnover cost example of $5,000 for a ten-dollar-per-hour employee, and an example turnover cost of $15,000 for a salaried employee, the following business case can be made:

Organizational Ratings

- Employees who rate their employer as "fair" or "poor" are 9.7 times more likely to look for a job within twelve months than those who rate their employer as "excellent." For every one hundred employees who move their organization ratings from "fair" or "poor" to "excellent," thirty-seven fewer employees would leave in the next year, amounting to $185,000 in savings for ten-dollar-per-hour employees and $555,000 in savings for salaried employees.

- Employees who rate their employer as "good" or "very good" are 2.8 times more likely to look for a job within twelve months than those who rate their employer as "excellent." For every one hundred employees who move their organization ratings from "good" or "very good" to "excellent," twenty-six fewer employees would leave in the next year, amounting to $130,000 in savings for ten-dollar-per-hour employees and $390,000 in savings for salaried employees.

Manager Ratings

- Employees who rate their manager as "fair" or "poor" are 7.6 times more likely to look for a job within twelve months than those who rate their manager as "excellent." For every one hundred employees who move their manager ratings from "fair" or "poor" to "excellent," twenty-one fewer employees would leave in the next year, amounting to $105,000 in savings for ten-dollar-per-hour employees and $315,000 in savings for salaried employees.

• Employees who rate their manager as "good" or "very good" are 2.3 times more likely to look for a job within twelve months than those who rate their manager as "excellent." For every one hundred employees who move their manager ratings from "good" or "very good" to "excellent," fourteen fewer employees would leave in the next year, amounting to $70,000 in savings for ten-dollar-per-hour employees and $210,000 in savings for salaried employees.

Growth and Development Ratings

• For every one hundred employees who move their growth and development ratings from "fair" or "poor" to "excellent," twenty-one fewer employees would leave in the next year, amounting to $105,000 in savings for ten-dollar-per-hour employees and $315,000 in savings for salaried employees.

• For every one hundred employees who move their growth and development ratings from "good" or "very good" to "excellent," fourteen fewer employees would leave in the next year, amounting to $70,000 in savings for ten-dollar-per-hour employees and $210,000 in savings for salaried employees.

Let's apply this on a larger scale: You have ten thousand employees. Based on the US average, 28 percent (2,800) of those employees will quit. With the average turnover cost at 33 percent of an employee's salary, and assuming your employees' average salary is $45,000, you will spend $14,850 per employee who leaves. That's $41.6 million for the 2,800 employees who will quit this year.

Now, as an example, let's look at one of the reasons those 2,800 people may leave: career development. Assume your employee data reports that 22 percent of employees who left (or intend to leave) is due to lack of career development. In your organization, that's 616 people, or $9.15 million in turnover expense. What if just half (308 employees) of those who left (or intend to leave) stayed or could be retained if you invested $400,000 in career development?

If you did nothing—made zero investment in retention—your annual turnover cost would still be $41.6 million. A four-hundred-thousand-dollar investment in retaining an additional 308 employees reduces your turnover cost to $37,006,200, reflecting an expense savings of more than $4.5 million. Subtracting the four-hundred-thousand-dollar investment, $4.1 million goes to the bottom line. And your turnover percentage is going in the right direction. Turnover is reduced from 28 percent to 25 percent. You are going in the right direction.

What's next?

You will still have turnover cost for the 78 percent of turnover reasons you didn't yet focus on, an additional $37 million savings opportunity. For each person you keep you are saving $14,850. Reducing your now 25 percent turnover another 10 percent will lower your turnover rate to 22.5 percent and save an additional $3.6 million.

 ## STOP AND THINK

Consider what you could save if you made investments in the many other reasons people leave organizations.

Using the above provided numbers, what if 11 percent of your people (1,100) are quitting or intend to quit because of poor supervisory behavior. That is a cost of more than $16 million.

Is there an ROI to your organization by intervening to address poor manager communication, unprofessionalism, lack of support, or unfairness?

Mock up a calculation. And remember: savings all go to the bottom line.

Employee turnover costs are on the rise as an employee-in-control marketplace intensifies, making it critical for organizations to proactively understand the intents of their workforce and prevent turnover to protect profits. When steps are taken to effectively understand employees and predict turnover, organizations can accurately identify segments of employees most likely to leave and the root causes of intent to stay or leave.

STOP AND THINK

Accounting systems of the last seventy-five years were built on models relevant to a manufacturing economy. However, as we have changed from a manufacturing economy to a human behavior economy, generally accepted accounting practices require reinvention.

Some companies make good attempts at suggesting "employees are their greatest assets." However, as long as employees are on the liability side of the balance sheet, they are not an asset.

- Perhaps it is time to figure out how to move employees over to the asset side of the balance sheet.

- Perhaps it is time to recognize that on-time, on-skill, and on-task employees enhance their value.

- Perhaps it is time to recognize that on-time, on-skill, and on-task employees enhance the company's value.

FIVE

THE EMPLOYER ENGAGEMENT MODEL: BECOMING A PREFERRED EMPLOYER

People in distress will sometimes prefer a problem that is familiar to a solution that is not.
—Neil Postman

Elizabeth Marshall, a young American, had traveled for miles across the Kalahari Desert with her family and several research scientists. . . . And then a young woman who appeared to be in her early twenties came out of the house.

"Presently she smiled, pressed her hand to her chest, and said: 'Tsetchwe.' It was her name.

"'Elizabeth,' I said, pointing to myself.

"'Nisabe,' she answered, pronouncing after me and inclining her head graciously. She looked me over carefully without really staring, which to Bushmen is rude. Then, having surely suspected that I was a woman, she put her hand on my breast gravely, and, finding that I was,

she gravely touched her own breast. Many Bushmen do this; to them all Europeans look alike.

"'Tsau si' (women), she said.

"Then after a moment's pause, Tsetchwe began to teach me a few words, the names of a few objects around us, grass, rock, bean, shell, so that we could have a conversation later. As she talked she took a handful of the beans out of her kaross, broke them open, and began to eat them."

"Tsetchwe began to teach me . . ." This is the essence of ethnography. Instead of collecting "data" about people, the ethnographer seeks to learn from people, to be taught by them.

"Tsetchwe began to teach me . . ." In order to discover the hidden principles of another way of life, the researcher must become the student. Tsetchwe, and those like her in every society, become teachers. Instead of studying the "climate," the "flora," and the "fauna" which make up the Bushmen's environment, Elizabeth Marshall tried to discover how the Bushmen define and evaluate drought and rainstorm, gemsbok and giraffe, torabe root and tsama melon. She did not attempt to describe Bushmen social life in terms of what we know as "marriage" or "family"; instead she sought to discover how Bushmen identified relatives and the cultural meaning of their kinship relationships. Discovering the insider's view is a different species of knowledge from one that rests primarily on the outsider's view. Even when the outsider is a trained social scientist.

(The previous is quoted directly from The Ethnographic Interview by James P. Spradley (Holt, Rinehart and Winston, 1979, pp. 3–4) including Spradley's use of quotes from The Harmless People by Elizabeth Marshall Thomas (New York: Random House, 1958.)

EMPLOYER ENGAGEMENT AND RETENTION REQUIRES A STRATEGIC APPROACH

In this economy, employees have options as the employment market-place is unchecked with job opportunities. Employees can choose environments wherein workplace conditions support their preferences. Regardless of an organization's mission, listening and responding to the workforce is necessary, and learning from the employee voice is an intentional, consistent, and continuous improvement requirement.

Collected and analyzed properly, an organization can possess the necessary information to diagnose, prescribe, remedy, and evaluate requirements. Managers can know employee intentions regarding staying or leaving, including what it would take for them to stay and why they really left.

As one allows improvement efforts to be guided by facts and data, there will be an impact. Immediate needs can be defined, resource requirements can be cost-benefitted, reasonable interventions can be executed, and improvements can be achieved.

STOP AND THINK

How would your company's climate improve if (1) you could identify reasons why employees left or intend to leave, and

(2) you acted on what you can do to increase length-of-stay?

EMPLOYER ENGAGEMENT: YOUR OPPORTUNITY

This section introduces key principles and methods to guide business productivity improvement with a focus on having on-time, on-board, and on-task employees. Sustainable success requires being able to attract and retain skilled employees, including managing the costs of attraction, retention, and productivity. Understanding employees' current and future requirements and acting on those requirements is core to attraction, retention, and engagement.

Key benefits for an organization to subscribe to an engaged employer model include

- increased employee contribution, satisfaction, and commitment;
- increased employee retention;
- enhanced employment brand;
- improved communication;
- enhanced employee capability;
- enhanced delivery of desired results to customers; and
- enhanced ability to anticipate and react to risks and vulnerabilities.

Whether an employer is large or small; centralized or in multiple geographies; product- or service-focused; for-profit, nonprofit, or in the government sector, becoming a Preferred and Engaged EmployER provides a framework for productivity improvement. As a business objective, the Preferred and Engaged EmployER model will help companies identify a strategy focused on employee requirements, business challenges, and business results.

EMPLOYER ENGAGEMENT PRINCIPLES

Principles are foundational to improving organizational performance and productivity. The following are fundamental to becoming a Preferred and Engaged EmployER:

- Principle 1: Attraction, retention, and engagement problems must be solved.

- Principle 2: Organizations must create a preferred place where current and future employees can exercise their occupational purpose.

- Principle 3: Collaborative approaches to decision-making identify employee preferences, expectations, and intents. Organizations must review and discuss employee feedback, identify priorities, and successfully work on defined problems/opportunities.

- Principle 4: Ongoing evidence-based actions are mutually beneficial to both employer and employee. Actions must be taken on evidence-based data to establish essential employer-employee trust.

- Principle 5: Transparent communications provide order, stability, and confidence. Sharing employee observations and improvements increases attractiveness, intent to stay/retention, and engagement.

- Principle 6: Organizations must track, report, and manage the costs of human behavior.

STOP AND THINK

Reread the Preferred and Engaged EmployER Principles.

Are these core philosophical beliefs of yours already?

What about your organization?

What needs to happen for your organization to subscribe to these principles?

EMPLOY**ER** ENGAGEMENT FOUNDATIONS

Foundational to EmployER Engagement is an organizational intent to become a better employer, a sound methodology, the recognition of key drivers, and action.

INTENT

An organization's intent (and success) in becoming a better employer requires the recognition of an employee-in-control workplace and an employee-centric approach to soliciting and identifying improvement requirements. Employees know what needs to be done to improve workplace conditions, business processes, and practices that enhance company performance and customer loyalty.

> If you give employees a voice and choose to listen, tremendous results can be realized. There is a somewhat famous story of the quest of a toothpaste company that wanted to increase sales. They decided to simply ask their employees for ideas. They expected to get selling and marketing ideas that would likely be advertising-centric. Much to their surprise, an employee came up with a brilliant yet simple and inexpensive strategy. Make the hole in the toothpaste tube bigger. The idea worked, and the increase in sales was significant.
>
> —Danny A. Nelms

METHODOLOGY

Methodology explains, guides, and directs how to carry out the specific activities, including a systematic approach in which employees express their views on the workplace conditions, including barriers to retention and engagement. As organizations request employee feedback, it is important that they do not limit the extent to which employees can express their experiences, ideas, and concerns. For example, asking employees to rate some aspect of the job on a 1–5 scale only tells part of the story. Whereas, if employees are given an opportunity to explain why they gave a particular rating, the organization receives more actionable data.

Research that incorporates both qualitative and quantitative methods provides more information than either method alone.[59] Quantitative data gives organizations a number representing how employees think or feel about a subject. Qualitative data provides insight as to why employees think or feel a particular way and the ways in which thoughts, feelings, and subsequent behaviors can be improved. Organizations can use feedback provided by employees to make necessary changes to organizational processes or policies across the stages of employment.[60] Ideally, employee voice is always gathered by an independent third party. Employee voice collected through internal tools often inhibits employees' ability to provide authentic responses for fear of retaliation or being singled out.

Organizations must implement an employee-centric research strategy that captures feedback at key stages of the employee experience, uses a reliable methodology to ask "why," and provides enough robust data for advanced analyses.[61]

KEY DRIVERS

There are four core areas of work around which employees form perceptions that drive engagement and retention behaviors. These include what the employee thinks or feels about the organization, the manager, the team, and the job itself.

ACTION

The actual change effort, this step derives from evidence determined in prior steps. This could include employee and manager development, career development, work-life-balance concerns, revision of specific practices and procedures, recognition and reward systems, or other specific change necessities.

EMPLOYER ENGAGEMENT MODEL

The EmployER Engagement Model explains, guides, and directs how to carry out specific activities. The following six steps are offered as the process to becoming a Preferred Employer.

STEP 1: PROBLEM/OPPORTUNITY IDENTIFICATION

The ratio of human capital expense relative to operating expenses is rising in many companies. Much of this is due to the increased costs related to activities that are controllable but not yet managed. In addition to not having the people necessary to do the work, other costs include extra training, hiring additional recruiters, agency fees, turnover, absenteeism, employee relation violations, and wage inflation.

The EmployER Engagement Model begins when key leadership recognizes that attraction, retention, and engagement can provide financial and brand value to the organization; that it is the right thing to do; and that problems can and must be solved.

In this phase, organization leadership typically identifies a core team tasked with developing the strategy to address targeted employee and related business issues. Clear goals are established, decision makers are identified, the team is empowered, resources are allocated, and communications commence.

The way you label a problem directs how you respond to it.

Setting the stage to compete for the best people, who will stay with the company, requires an open and public broadcast of the company's commitment to increasingly become a better employer. Critical to this stage, the employer articulates its promise and the plan for its unique EmployER Engagement Journey.

Tasks for the selected committee include managing communications and defining outcome goals and objectives aligned with organizational needs. Objectives worthy of consideration might include increasing attraction, as evidenced by increases in job inquiries and applications; improving employee selection, as evidenced by increases in new-hire evaluations; increases in intent-to-stay measures; decreases in the instances and costs of absenteeism; decreases in the costs of turnover; reductions in the size of the recruitment department; and reduction in employee litigation, litigation threat, and ethics violations.

STEP 2: THE EMPLOYEE VOICE

Too many organizations try to address retention with others' best practices or compromised data, and fail to understand the real reasons employees stay or leave. Responsible studies, using appropriate methodology and timing, allow employees to reveal the real, root causes of turnover, turnover intent, and other targeted concerns. Managers can have a sense of employee intention regarding plans and timing to stay or leave, and an understanding of why they will stay and why they will leave.

> A friend and colleague, Kelley O'Brien, is a talent acquisition professional in a large health-care organization. She tells the story about how she is deluged by all the commercial study results that come across her desk. The benefits company that used to regularly send cookies now sends her study results proving that engagement is uniquely tied to increased benefits, while the employee recognition company that used to send over donuts now sends research study results that guarantee improved engagement with plaques, hats, and golf shirts. The staffing firm that used to deliver stress balls now has study results on how managed contract labor can solve all her engagement problems.
>
> Kelley, a skilled researcher herself, knows better. She recently commented: "Data are the new donuts." However, a donut is preferable to bad data.
>
> —Thomas F. Mahan

Time is to be lived now, not in the past. In order to make information actionable, it needs to be current and available "just in time." Within hours of obtaining information from respondents, an organization's database must be updated. Within seconds of obtaining information about a specific "flagged" issue (e.g., interest in being rehired, fraud, abuse, or illegal or unethical issues), alerts must be "pushed" to designated representatives in the organization. Immediate follow-up is possible and necessary.

Learning from employees is an intentional, continuous improvement process.

There are multiple ways to collect the employee voice. Decisions on which feedback tool(s) to use depends on the current needs of the employer. For example, if the company objective is to reduce turnover with first-year employees, an onboarding study and an exit study with less than thirteen-month employee quits is recommended. If the business objective is to reduce turnover in a specific region or role, a stay study and an exit study with that region or role should be considered. Should the employer objective be to establish a baseline of satisfaction, an annual study should be considered, perhaps followed up with a quarterly role or region-targeted stay study. An employer may want to consider including a behavior risk study as an affirmative tool to identify and eliminate problems. Additional information on intentional studies directed at helping an organization identify actions necessary to become a preferred employer follows.

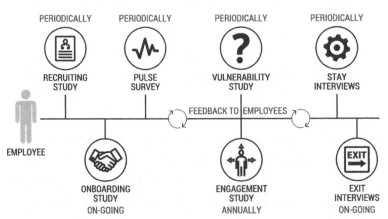

ONBOARDING STUDY

First-year turnover is at its highest point in the past eight years. The rise in first-year turnover is a sign of the job market, as employees can easily go elsewhere if their current role doesn't immediately meet their preferences and expectations.

About half of employees who leave during year one do so within the first ninety days. If an employee makes it past the ninety-day mark, there is still a 20 percent chance he or she will quit before the end of the year.

Onboarding is the period in which new employees acquire the necessary knowledge, skills, and behaviors to become effective members of teams, departments, and organizations. As research links effective onboarding to reduced turnover and increased retention,[62] the onboarding period is a critical time to assist new hires with adjustment to the social and performance aspects of their role. Studies show that effective onboarding reduces the time it takes a new employee to effectively contribute to the organization.[63] Benefits of a shortened ramp-up time include reduced time to reach productivity, achievement of better performance, and establishment of workplace relationships. The Corporate Leadership Council found that effective onboarding increases employees' "discretionary effort" by as much as 20 percent.[64] Research additionally links effective onboarding to improved employee perceptions of workplace conditions.[65] The immediate benefit of effective onboarding is a productive new hire. The longer-term benefit includes retention.

First-year quits accounted for 40 percent of all turnover in 2017, up from 34 percent in 2016.

An onboarding study, sometimes referred to as "new-hire surveys," is a research tool through which employers regularly request feedback from new employees about the onboarding process. The intent of using the onboarding study is to understand what can be improved within the entry process to help new hires become productive in their role, effectively assimilate, and stay longer. An onboarding study can reveal information on

- the effectiveness of each stage of onboarding;
- how to improve each stage of onboarding;
- current attitudes around workplace conditions that drive satisfaction and retention;
- the effectiveness of job training elements;
- new employee intent to stay with the company; and
- organizational behavioral risks.

Employee feedback can be solicited from new hires after orientation, after the first day on the job, after thirty days on the job, after ninety days on the job, and periodically thereafter. However, to make this data meaningful and action-focused, employers should schedule onboarding study solicitation points timed to when it's most impactful to the period that employers risk losing employees. For example, should the highest frequency of turnover for new hires occur at the six-month point, a study should be scheduled at the time of hire and the three- or four-month mark. This provides intervention time for the employer to identify conditions that drive quits, communicate awareness of the concern, and implement actions to be taken to save at-risk employees. A final measure may take place toward the end of the onboarding period, perhaps at the eleven-month mark.

To ensure accuracy, onboarding studies should be conducted by an independent, objective third party to remove bias and any barriers possibly preventing employees from expressing their true perceptions of their employment relationship. When internally conducted, intent disclosure is often compromised as employees may be concerned about anonymity.

To obtain detailed perceptions of the onboarding period and how to improve it, as with most employee-centric research, a mixed methodology that asks why in an open-ended, drill-down manner to secure the most comprehensive information is recommended. Outside, objective third-party researchers can offer high-quality telephonic interviews and web interviews to capture in-depth quantitative and qualitative responses. Probing questions provide details on opportunities to improve the onboarding process and positively impact employees' experiences.

To ensure participation, trust, and action, the results (strengths and weaknesses) of the onboarding study must be communicated back to the employees, as well as thanking them for their participation and informing them of any changes that will be implemented and when.

Questions in an onboarding study can be tailored to the activities and desired outcomes of that unique employment situation. In addition to unique employer-specific measures, onboarding studies should ask open-ended questions to assess the employee's thoughts and feelings about

- the organization;
- their team;
- their manager;
- their job;
- the onboarding process;
- the training received;

- what it will take to get "excellent" ratings;

- how long the employee intends to stay and why;

- what it would take to increase length-of-stay; and

- awareness of unethical, fraudulent, safety, or behavioral issues that might compromise the employee's role or the company.

Onboarding studies provide multiple benefits to organizations, including improving the onboarding experience, identifying the key drivers of satisfaction, building community, improving new-hire training, uncovering and acting on potential behavior risks, speeding up time-to-productivity, and retention.

THE ANNUAL EMPLOYEE STUDY

The annual employee study has become a common tool used to solicit feedback from employees and (when properly conducted) to inform strategies to improve the employee and employer relationship.

Over the last decade, an emphasis has been placed on measuring employee engagement in the organization, as it has been argued that employee engagement levels are linked to business outcomes such as customer satisfaction, employee turnover, productivity, and profits.[66]

The popularity of employee engagement has led service, product, and survey companies to specify their own definitions and measures. Sometimes the questions are just a rebranding of historical satisfaction, loyalty, and commitment studies, where the employer is asking employees to rate items that have been used in the past (e.g., scaled ratings of compensation, benefits, supervisors, work environment, and communication). In many cases, the questions asked actually manipulate the answers to point to products and services offered by the survey provider. Faulty employee studies do not provide adequate and accurate information for organizations to make meaningful improvements, perhaps most evidenced by the fact that engagement scores rarely go up.

> *"If you do not know how to ask the right question, you discover nothing."*
> —W. Edwards Deming

Regardless of how an annual employee study is labeled, employers can increase productivity through reduced human-capital costs, increased productive output, employee retention, and reduced costs of inappropriate behaviors. To do so, employers must focus on the conditions created in the workplace that reinforce (or extinguish) employee perceptions (thoughts and feelings), and resultant behaviors. Properly conducted, the annual employee study helps an organization

- understand perceptions around workplace conditions;
- establish a baseline from which to improve;
- secure insights for guiding efforts to improve;
- assess intent to stay and intent to leave; and
- uncover and act on actual and potential compliance concerns.

To ensure accuracy, the annual study should be coproduced between employees and an independent third party. This reduces employee resistance to expressing their perceptions on workplace conditions.[67] When conducted internally, true intents and root causes are not fully revealed.

Obtaining actionable intelligence to improve productivity requires exploring and understanding employee perceptions of workplace conditions. A mixed methodology, supporting both quantitative and qualitative probes, increases what can be learned from employees. Third-party researchers can offer telephonic interviews and web interviews to capture in-depth responses and can identify action items to improve the employment environment. Questions should be open-ended inquiries about the organization, team, manager and the job itself.

- How does the employee feel about the organization?
- How does the employee feel about their team?
- How does the employee feel about their manager?
- How does the employee feel about their job?
- What will it take to get excellent ratings on key workplace conditions?
- What is the employee's intent to stay/intent to leave, when, and what needs to be different?
- Awareness of any compliance issue? Where and when?

The annual study helps the employer identify specific opportunities that require intervention; align effective evidence-based retention solutions; identify turnover risk; and identify, reduce, and eliminate compliance issues that place the organization at risk.

Exit Study

The final stage of employment in an organization, the exit, is a critical time to collect feedback from employees. An internal exit interview with the soon-to-be-former employee is a way to update contact information, collect keys, parking pass and ID, complete benefits information, and wish the employee well in his or her new role. This is also an opportunity for the employer to converse with the employee about his/her work experience, why he/she is leaving, and what the company might do to be a better employer. This final interview is also a time to reestablish rapport with the employee, should there be opportunity for reconsideration or eventual rehire presently or later.

While it is appropriate (and important) to interview the employee regarding reasons for leaving, the employer must exercise caution in acting on information received. Repeated studies demonstrate that reasons provided for quitting at time of termination to an internal person are not representative of actual reasons. Indeed, 63 percent of answers change by having a third party ask about reasons for leaving after the employee has departed.[68] Should employers choose to intervene on reasons provided at point of termination, they are at risk of intervening in the wrong areas.

> *"Defects are not free. Somebody makes them, and gets paid for making them."*
> —W. Edwards Deming

As less than 8 percent of employers share a common turnover profile, nearly every organization is unique in the reasons employees quit. This underscores the importance of exit studies as foundational to an effective retention strategy.[69] An externally conducted exit study, whether with an individual or with a collective of former employees, done properly, reveals the true causes of turnover and provides an employer with insight to drive actions to improve retention. For example, allowing former employees to voice their concerns about their former managers and direct supervisors can provide the organization with insight on how to improve the behavior and leadership of managers.[70] In general, exit studies provide an opportunity for former employees to explain why they left and the ways they think their former organization could be improved.[71] The organization can act on this information to improve employee retention.[72]

To learn the real reasons employees leave, and make decisions to remediate those reasons, leaders need to ask why they left in a way that gets to the truth. Employers can

- identify the real reasons employees left;

- accurately identify opportunities for improvement;

- understand attitudes around workplace conditions;

- develop targeted strategies to prevent turnover;

- discover what it would take to win employees back;

- uncover potential behavior risk concerns; and

- secure competitive information on where former employees went to work and why.

To ensure accuracy and meaningfulness, and to drive correct solutions, employers should use an outside, objective third party to conduct the exit study. When conducted internally, it's likely that true intents and root causes related to retention aren't revealed because employees aren't being honest with their managers; they are merely filling out a procedural form, or they provide the politically correct reason. For example, a soon-to-be-former employee may report, "I'm leaving for more money." In this case, acting on the wrong reason risks increased expenses with wage inflation. When exit studies are conducted by a third party, versus the organization itself, the reasons employees give for why they left are different.[73] Additionally, when open-ended questions are asked, organizations gain greater insight into employee experiences.[74]

Total separations are comprised of voluntary (employee-initiated) and involuntary (employer-directed) quits. All former employees (voluntary and involuntary terminations) should be studied so employers understand why all people leave and what needs to be different for all people to stay. Individual and comprehensive data can be analyzed to identify issues that exist in specific employee segments (e.g., departments, job groups, supervisors) or with individual personalities.

Questions in an exit study focus on the organization, team, manager, and job. Reasons for turnover need to be explored.

- How does the employee feel about the organization?
- How does the employee feel about his or her former team?
- How does the employee feel about his or her former manager?
- How does the employee feel about his or her former job?
- What are the *real* reasons the employee left the organization?
- What was the most important reason the employee left?
- Where did the employee go to work and why?
- What it would take to get the former employee to reconsider return? Is he or she interested in return?
- Is the employee aware of any unethical, illegal, behavioral, or financial impropriety? Where and when?

Ongoing exit studies provide multiple benefits to employers. Employers can identify specific solutions to improve retention, build a pipeline of former employees who would return, and reduce or eliminate behavioral incidents that put the organization and employees at risk.

In many cases, employers can view exited employee observations as representative of the employees who remain. Understanding the experiences of former employees enables companies to make the right changes to improve conditions for current employees, helping them choose to stay longer.

STAY STUDY

Organizations can know the truth about why employees chose to stay and predict and minimize employee loss risk. An effective Preferred and Engaged EmployER strategy includes a stay study to understand the workplace conditions that drive retention and turnover.[75] Properly conducted, a stay study delivers insights to improve retention by predicting quits and providing action guidance to reduce turnover and increase retention.

The reasons employees stay at an organization are different from the reasons they leave.

A stay study includes telephonic or web-based one-on-one interviews with current employees by an outside, objective researcher. A stay study can be used with full employee populations or with at-risk employee segments, such as specific roles or locations, or other vulnerable populations (e.g., highly marketable, unsatisfied employees). These segments of employees could also include top-performing employees, high-potential employees, those employees in the succession plan, highly skilled technical workers, key sales professionals, workers who live in low-unemployment markets, and more. The overall objective of conducting a stay study is to provide insight into the intents of employees to stay or leave with details to identify interventions that will increase retention. Employers can

- uncover the most important reasons employees stay;
- discover WHEN employees intend to leave;
- understand WHY employees intend to leave;
- understand WHAT needs to be done to increase length-of-stay;

- intervene with targeted interventions based on employee recommendations;
- proactively reduce turnover; and
- proactively uncover and act on potential risk concerns.

Stay studies, used as a piece of a fuller employee research plan, inform employers with employee feedback throughout the employee life cycle. While measuring and understanding employees' perceptions of their work environment with a one-time study provides a baseline from which to improve, assuming results represent employee perceptions throughout the year is a mistake. Employers, following a baseline study, are encouraged to request, secure, and act on employee feedback periodically in order to assess, identify, and remediate or develop intent-to-stay strengths, intent-to-leave weaknesses, and solutions to lessen the loss of intent-to-leave.

An employer is advised to audit and know when exactly turnover occurs, and intervene with stay studies a couple of months prior to employee quit trends. Additionally, as the employer assesses potential turnover vulnerability, perhaps due to a planned new employer moving into the geography or a merger/acquisition effort, a stay study can identify quit risk, and the employer can take necessary action to limit employee loss.

As with other employee studies, to ensure sufficient responses and accuracy, stay studies should be conducted by an outside, objective third party. When conducted internally, true intentions and root causes related to intent to stay and intent to leave often do not identify real concerns.

Inaccurate results place the organization at risk of intervening in the wrong area, thus increasing expenses with compromised results.

To obtain detailed reasons for intent to stay and intent to leave, a mixed methodology with open-ended questions is the best approach, informing the real reasons why employees think or feel the way they do and what the employer can do about it. Asking increases the power to predict intent to stay by 20 percent.[76] To understand specific actions that could move employees' ratings of organization, team, manager, and job to "excellent," it is also necessary to ask what it would take to get a top rating. Acting on probing questions provides the required details necessary to improve the employment relationship, positively impact the employee's experience, and extend employee length-of-stay.

To ensure continued participation, trust, and organization improvement, the results (strengths and weaknesses) of stay studies must be shared with the employees, as well as thanking them for their insights and recommendations and informing employees what will be implemented and when. As employers typically cannot make massive changes all at one time, employers additionally need to inform employees what will not be implemented at this time, why, and when it will be revisited.

Stay study questions focus on the organization, team, manager, and job. Other known or hypothesized issues aligned with retention challenges or employee concerns can also be tested and those results explored. As with other employee-centric research, stay studies should focus on asking open-ended questions about the key conditions that effect retention and satisfaction.

- How does the employee feel about the organization; what would it take to get an "excellent" rating?
- How does the employee feel about the team? What would it take to get an "excellent" rating?
- How does the employee feel about the manager? What would it take to get an "excellent" rating?

- How does the employee feel about his or her job? What would it take to get an "excellent" rating?

- How long does the employee plan to stay with the organization? What would be required to increase length-of-stay?

- What is the most important issue driving the employee's intent to stay with the organization, or what is the most important issue driving the employee's intent to leave the organization?

Stay studies benefit organizations by identifying at-risk employees and at-risk employee segments, informing actions necessary to increase length-of-stay.

RECRUITMENT STUDY

Given current workforce economics, the ability to attract the employees necessary to do the work that needs to be done is vital. Many recruitment processes today, however, meet mostly legacy and administrative objectives, with little regard to potential employee relationships. Applicant tracking systems and artificial intelligence tools for searching résumés may be efficiency tools for the employer, but often significantly diminish the potential employee experience.

Employers must understand the impact of the recruitment process on candidates. Organizations can know the truth about why employees chose to accept employment offers or chose to decline those same offers.

Employers must ensure their recruiting practices are securing the employees they need.

A recruitment study includes telephonic or web-based one-on-one interviews with recently hired employees, and those who rejected a job offer. Employers can:

- understand the real reasons employees accept offers;

- uncover the most important causes for offer declines;

- discover specific and actionable ways to improve acceptance rates and quality of hires; and

- know what it would take to get offer acceptances.

Recruitment studies benefit organizations by identifying the recruitment concerns that put candidates at risk to decline the job offer.

PULSE STUDY

Utilized properly, a pulse study provides an effective, just-in-time tool to obtain quick feedback on organizational issues and the effectiveness of workplace interventions. Unlike other studies in the EmployER Engagement model, a simple survey approach with ratings-only responses is acceptable. Pulse studies can be quick, simple, and instructive.

There are three primary uses for pulse surveys:

1. Tracking perceptions of workplace interventions: The EmployER Engagement Model includes the development and implementation of specific actions aimed at improving workplace conditions. An organization need not wait lengthy periods of time to determine if certain changes are having the intended effect. Utilizing pulse studies is an effective tool to quickly ask employees to provide evaluative feedback.

2. Receiving feedback on organizational changes: Organizations change quickly, and employee experience feedback on certain changes can be very useful in identifying issues

that must be addressed. Examples could include leadership changes, shifts in business strategy, mergers or acquisitions, total reward changes, additional communication requirements, or other organization decisions that influence employee perceptions and behavior.

3. Just plain fun: Sometimes organizations just need to interject a little fun in the engagement experience. Pulse surveys can ask, "Which team is going to win the Super Bowl?" "Is it ham or turkey for holiday traditions?" or "Who is your favorite Disney character?"

As a reminder, it is important to keep in mind that pulse surveys, like any other voice of the employee research event, require the organization to communicate what employees said and what, if anything, the organization is going to do.

ETHICS-, FRAUD-, AND BEHAVIOR-VULNERABILITY STUDY

Preventing and managing misconduct is an organizational imperative for employers, investors, board members, regulators, and others interested in running, protecting, evaluating, and valuing an organization. In today's world of text messaging, mobile phone cameras, and social media, organizations are increasingly vulnerable because of the availability of instant public broadcast of misconduct.

Employers are at risk for behaviors that have become normalized as part of individual personalities (e.g., "That's just the way she is," "Boys will be boys," or "He just does that because he cares so much about everyone."); and for behaviors that have been accepted as part of the culture (e.g., betrayals, bad management, silent yet complicit observers of inappropriate behavior, broken promises, and theft).

"The price of light is less than the cost of darkness."
—Arthur C. Nielsen

Given the considerable reputational and financial risk associated with workplace misconduct, organizations have implemented initiatives to help discourage incidents of misbehavior. However, while much guidance comes from the federal sentencing guidelines, by the time a problem gets to that point it is often too late. As typical models for compliance reporting are passive and reactive, current systems and programs for discovering and reporting reliable information about improper conduct in the workplace, in a timely manner, are largely failing. Rather than affirmatively seeking out questionable behaviors, companies seem to wait for noncompliance and unethical behaviors to be reported by employees. In some cases, employers only act at the point of post-employment class action suits.

Despite the numerous 2017 and 2018 very public reports of celebrity sexual harassment, few employers are acting to address the sexual harassment problem. A recent study by the American Psychological Association Center for Organizational Excellence shows that only 32 percent of working Americans report their employers have taken new steps to address and report sexual harassment; only 18 percent have reminded employees of existing policies; only 10 percent have added new training or resources; a mere 8 percent have strengthened their policy; and 78 percent said they are now more likely to report it if they experience it.[77]

Ongoing research from the Work Institute indicates that up to 6 percent of former employees were aware of some type of misconduct in the workplace yet did not report it to the organization while they were employed.

Organizations seem to be effective in training employees about compliance. Missing, but necessary, is an effective vehicle with which employees can report misconduct, and training for supervisors in recognizing and responding to aberrant behavior. Employers can affirmatively address issues before they escalate out of control. With proactive reporting systems, behavior-based interviewing techniques, and appropriate and timely response to misbehavior, employers can create a safer and more attractive work climate.

Additionally, top-down organizational messaging is mandatory in any effort to manage, reduce, and eliminate workplace misconduct. Throughout the employment life cycle, it is vital that employees are aware of the importance of conducting business in a principled manner. Orientation, training, and reporting all play an essential role in creating a workplace free of inappropriate behavior. To encourage reporting of incidents, employees must learn that employers expect proper conduct, will act accordingly, and will do something about misconduct.

According to the Equal Employment Opportunity Commission (EEOC), the number-one reason given by employees for NOT reporting noncompliant and unethical conduct is the fear of discovery and subsequent reprisal. When the assurance of anonymity is provided, employees are considerably more comfortable disclosing experienced, observed, and rumored misconduct. Employees who report workplace misconduct are taking a risk. They want to be comfortable that the systems being utilized to report misconduct protect their identity.

The procedures an organization implements to encourage, monitor, assess, report, and manage misconduct are crucial to organizational and compliance program effectiveness. Criminal incidents and unethical practices cripple productivity and create mounting costs associated with turnover, fines, investigations, and brand. Governance, risk management, and compliance initiatives need to shift away from exclusively passive suggestion boxes and costly and underutilized

1-800 compliance lines. By the time the incident reaches management, the damage has already been done.

Affirmative and preemptive tactics, such as asking employees specifically if they are aware of any unethical, illegal, fraudulent, or inappropriate behavior, offer far more advantages than passive and voluntary means of reporting. It is in everyone's best interest (employer and employees) for an organization to solicit reports of misconduct.

Utilizing telephonic and web-based interviews, companies can proactively and routinely solicit and document awareness (and the lack thereof) of illegal, unethical, and noncompliant behavior in their workforce. Key probes to include when surveying include "Are you aware of any unethical, illegal, financial impropriety, or inappropriate behavior? Where and when? Please describe."

When employees take the risk of reporting unwanted or unethical behaviors, it is reasonable that they expect some action will be taken. Definitive action following an employee report is key to encouraging and increasing the likelihood that employees will report misconduct that puts the employee and the employer at risk in the future. If employees routinely report their awareness of workplace misconduct and do not see action or do not have a means to obtain feedback on the actions taken, they are unlikely to take additional risks to report concerns. Providing a mechanism to obtain feedback on actions increases the likelihood of affirmative reporting.

While not the primary reason for conducting ongoing risk studies, it is additionally advantageous to the employer to collect, report, and manage responses of "Not aware." In some cases, as a current or former employee files a claim or suggests that the company didn't intervene when it should have, the company needs to be able to ascertain whether the employee did indeed report the behavior or alternatively reported "Not aware." This can be an important defense strategy.

An ethics-, fraud-, and behavior-vulnerability study does not need to be an independent study. Vulnerability questions can be added to other employee-centric studies. For example, added to the stay study, the question becomes, "I just have one more question to ask you. Please understand that, unless ordered by a court of law, your name will not be associated with your response. Are you aware of any unethical, illegal, or financial impropriety or inappropriate behaviors?" If not, thank the employee and end the interview. If so, say, "Please describe. Where and when did this occur?"

Reports of unethical, illegal, or financial impropriety or inappropriate behaviors must be immediately and readily available to employee relations or the legal team for triage, investigation, and determination of next steps.

Strengths are also important. An opportunity exists for companies to start looking at ethics and compliance through a strength-based lens. While traditional programs are violation- and problem-focused, companies can collect, report, and celebrate ethical, behavioral, and compliance good news. A "good news" question can also be included in an ethics and compliance study: "Are you aware of any exceptional things anyone has done to support ethical behavior?" It is also appropriate to ask if employees are aware of individuals who went above and beyond in supporting the organization's values. Additional strength data includes reporting the percentage of employees who are not aware of any unethical, illegal, or financial impropriety. This can be tracked over time and celebrated as the percentage increases.

STOP AND THINK

How would your company improve if you could proactively identify behavioral, financial, ethical, and legal risks and respond before people, financials, brand, and safety are compromised?

STEP 3: ANALYSIS

At this step, employer leadership, operations, and HR review the results of targeted studies and identify the strengths and weaknesses of where turnover, turnover intent, and disengagement are at risk. This phase includes the review and discussion of employee feedback, candid discussions on the willingness and readiness of the organization to work on identified problems, the identification and prioritization of actions, and communication requirements and opportunities.

Two outputs result at this level. First, if appropriate to the assessment results, the employer starts holding managers accountable for the retention and engagement of employees who choose to work in their units. When adding retention accountability to performance objectives, managers and supervisors are more likely to lend additional attention to employees. Second, the workforce receives continuous communication regarding survey results, the actions to be taken, when the actions will be taken, and how those actions are aligned with the information employees provided.

Remember: The key isn't doing the study. It is doing the right things with the results.

There are five major targets to consider in problem-solving, corrective action, cost management, and planning. These areas include organization-wide issues, unit-specific issues, competitive intelligence, re-recruitment, and risk management/affirmative responsibility.

Organization-wide issues cut across all or most organizational units. Included in this category might be issues related to mission, vision, and values, such as trust in upper management and issues of organizational identity—who we are, what we do.

Typically, senior management, a centralized organization-effectiveness function, or the Preferred and Engaged EmployER Committee will address issues in this category, as effective interventions frequently benefit from a coordinated and focused effort or require the investment of organization-wide resources. For this category, most improvement efforts tend to be top-down (e.g., issues of organizational identity; creating and implementing new development programs; skill-based pay, policy, and procedure revisions; or the creation of specific career paths).

Role/location-specific issues aren't always relevant to most or all work units. Communication and intervention at the unit level are frequently best driven by unit managers in collaboration with employees. This is a bottom-up approach in which the unit uses the analyzed results to identify and communicate focused objectives, decides and communicates accountability and timeline, and defines cost-benefit. Resultant plans are formally communicated to ensure accountability.

Competitive intelligence is based on responsibly collected information about where and why employees are going and when they leave or intend to leave the organization. This information helps determine and construct intervention requirements for attraction and retention.

Re-recruitment/recommitment of current and former employees and former applicants is based on specific questions: whether former employees (or applicants) would be interested in returning to the organization, what needs to occur to re-recruit/recommit existing employees, and what it would take for former employees/current employees/applicants to reconsider the organization. Action steps here are straightforward. The first step is usually to determine whether the organization is interested in having/keeping the employee. If the answer is yes, the next step is to talk to the person and begin the re-attraction process. Re-recruitment strategies of former applicants, current employees, and former employees are constructed based on employee feedback.

Risk management/affirmative responsibility data must be triaged and acted upon quickly before the organization finds itself in a costly defense situation.

STEP 4: ACCOUNTABILITY, MANAGEMENT, ACTION

The value of data lies in using it for improvement. This stage is the actual change effort and is based on evidence determined in prior steps. Three things are essential to effective action. First, without management commitment, systemic and durable change will not result. Second, supervisors and managers must be held accountable for engagement and retention. Finally, there needs to be a publicly posted written plan that is shared and monitored for accountability. The plan must establish objectives (action and outcome), identify person(s) responsible for doing what by when (i.e., the actual intervention); identify resource requirements to implement the intervention; monitor implementation; and communicate findings, actions, evaluation, and revisions.

Intervening on retention and engagement requires accountability at all levels in the organization. Action planning is a bottom-up process focused on valid employee-voice data, and clear actions and accountabilities must be managed. Organizations, and most locations, are different. To be successful, companies must operate out of their own unique evidence-based action requirements. Action items could include member (employee, supervisor, manager) career development, work-life-balance policies, practices and procedures, job characteristics, recognition and reward systems, or structural changes, such as the actual work environment, among others.

CAREER DEVELOPMENT

Career development includes opportunities for growth, achievement, and security. Employees increasingly are aware of the need to take control of their careers, a control they can manage with their current employers or elsewhere. As career opportunities increase, employers must take steps to understand the needs, preferences, and goals of their workers or miss out on opportunities to keep workers that they need.

A good starting point for employee career development is helping employees assess, learn, and develop their own career plans. Career tests in the areas of occupational personality, values, skill motivation, and interests can help employees learn about their vocational self-concept, including who they are occupationally, where and how they do their best work, and with whom they do their best work. Career counselors can assist employees in identifying and learning about occupational alternatives at the company, understanding the process—including preparation and skill development requirements for selected alternatives—and implementing vocational choice. Customized career plans can be developed to include project work, stretch assignments, mentors, or temporary roles and projects.

If career development is an evidence-based retention requirement, career counselors may be helpful to employer and employee objectives. Business-focused career counselors, internal or external, can assist employees by

- helping them understand their occupational personalities, interests, and values;
- helping them identify and overcome barriers to career development;
- helping them navigate employee development opportunities;
- encouraging interests and personal identities beyond their occupation;
- providing instructional counseling/coaching to help employees accelerate competence in specific skill areas such as col-

laboration, empathy, rapport, conflict management, problem-solving, and critical thinking; and

- addressing employee concerns through information, liaison and coordination services, and referrals.

Further, business-focused career counselors can assist employers by

- supporting cultural and behavioral change in areas where management style and operating culture increase workplace stress;
- determining employee selection criteria, thorough assessing, interviewing, and providing feedback;
- training managers to recognize aberrant behavior;
- providing advice and counseling to cope with conflicts that emerge from differing worldviews in the workplace;
- facilitating new manager assimilation; and
- facilitating succession planning and development.

As new-to-work employees often have little understanding of expected behaviors, there may be benefit in minimizing some of the pitfalls they are likely to face. Basic early-career professional skills, knowledge, and attitudes can be part of a career development curriculum that assists new employee success. Key content might include the following:

- Punctuality and attendance: "on time" defined, awareness of attendance and tardiness policies
- Information about unwritten rules: the organization's mission and vision and values, what behaviors are expected as a result

- Attitude and the part it plays in the workplace: how to show respect to coworkers and managers, how to challenge with respect

- Confidence and the courage to ask questions: how to ask for help or clarification

- Self-awareness: behavior styles

- Personal brand: what people expect in themselves

- Presentation skills (basic): preparing and delivering a presentation (project update, committee report, etc.)

- Personal image: handshake, speaking up, dress, personal hygiene

- Meeting etiquette: attentive, focused, respectful, not on phone or other device

- Goal/expectation setting

- Presence at workday

- Communication elements: basics of an appropriate email, text, conversation

- Ethical behavior

- Appropriate language

- Representing the company

Many new supervisors and managers are promoted because of strong technical skills, but they lack some of the necessary social behaviors required in their new roles. Given turnover and intent-to-leave measures, new supervisors and managers may benefit from basic professionalism career development. Topics covered in a new-manager professionalism curriculum will likely include the following:

- Building trust: keeping one's word

- Perceptions of fairness
- Supportive attitude: managing to help employees improve
- Demeanor: courtesy, difficult conversations, appropriate display of emotions
- Communication skills: verbal, written
- Managing teams: understanding team dynamics
- Image: language, appearance, interaction with others
- Ethical behavior: role model for what's appropriate

WORK-LIFE BALANCE

Employee travel, commute, scheduling, and schedule-flexibility preferences tend to construct the work-life-balance category. Some employees would like to increase travel; some prefer to reduce it. Paramount to the employment relationship is a supervisor who knows these preferences. As the demand for workers grows, employers must understand how they can offer more favorable conditions to attract and retain employees. Employers can design ways to improve other conditions within their organizations to make them preferred by workers. Work-from-home options and early-in-early-out, late-in-late-out, and split schedules, if supported by your employee preferences, may all be worthy considerations.

MANAGER BEHAVIOR

Manager behavior concerns primarily are described as unprofessionalism, lack of support, poor treatment of employees, generally poor behavior, poor communication, lack of manager competence, and lack of manager fairness.

Employees are likely to go elsewhere to get what they expect in a supervisor if their manager doesn't demonstrate acceptable behavior. Employers must ensure managers are well trained in their relationship skills and conduct or continue to pay the price through employee turnover. Organizations are advised to revisit their current training programs to verify that the supervisor and manager practices expected and taught align with current requirements.

Areas of critical focus for supervisors and mid-level managers might include fairness; supportive attitudes; helping employees improve; courtesy; being able to conduct difficult conversations; communication, including writing, talking, and listening skills; and understanding of individual, team, and group dynamics; language; appearance; and ethical behavior.

Skill, knowledge, and attitudinal behavior requirements may include the following:

- Coaching with emotional intelligence
- "Teamness," including collaboration among peers and with supervisors
- Change management: understanding and communicating personal, group, and leadership practices at each stage of the change cycle
- Communications
- Business writing
- Presentation skills
- Finance for nonfinancial managers
- Dealing with difficult situations, including the importance of immediacy
- Professional image, including ethical behavior

WELL-BEING

Well-being includes personal and organizational practices and policies related to physical, emotional, and family-related concerns, including personal health, caregiver concerns, pregnancy, and family issues. Employers who do not actively pay attention to their workers' needs to take care of themselves and their families will see turnover. It's critical to understand the challenges that employees face and work with them to accommodate special needs.

COMPENSATION AND BENEFITS

Employers must increasingly become concerned about the role of pay and benefits in employee retention. While Work Institute studies show that less than one in ten employees leave for compensation and benefits reasons, an organization needs to know how they specifically affect employee reasons for staying or leaving. Often the real issue is one of perceived fairness in total rewards received and total rewards promised. Another consideration is whether compensation is competitive in the local environment.

JOB CHARACTERISTICS

Employers must get better at providing realistic job previews. Necessary to attraction, recruitment, and retention, a realistic job preview communicates the good and bad aspects of a job, providing applicants with honest and accurate views of what a job entails. Thoroughly understanding the work environment, duties, schedules, and other expectations helps the applicant evaluate if he or she is a good match. A realistic job-preview self-assessment goes hand in hand with traditional organization tools such as experience records, references, interviews, and screening assessments (e.g., cognitive, ability, personality, and interpersonal testing instruments).

WORK ENVIRONMENT

The upward trend of the work environment category shows that, in general, many employers are not doing enough to understand and improve conditions that could prevent turnover. If problematic from the employee perspective, employers must do all they can to improve this area. Employees are increasingly less tolerant of poor physical facilities, unsafe or hazardous environments, and toxic behaviors from supervisors and coworkers, especially when better conditions are available elsewhere.

STEP 5: CONTINUOUS COMMUNICATIONS

Sharing employee observations and employer commitments to improvements can increase applicant attractiveness and employee intent to stay, retention, and engagement. An ongoing effort, the Preferred and Engaged EmployER Model requires personal communications and public postings on the organizational commitment to increasingly become a better employer.

"My idea of good company . . . is the company of clever, well-informed people who have a great deal of conversation; that is what I call good company."
"You are mistaken," said he, gently. "That is not good company, that is the best."
—Jane Austen, *Persuasion*

There are several internal and external foci for continuous communication.

Employee Communication

Employers must reiterate the value they place on employee feedback, thank employees for their feedback, and transparently and quickly share study results. Additionally, companies must share how and why change priorities were determined, inform employees about changes they may experience, and announce dates and milestones for action implementation.

Employee communications can be distributed through regular company channels and debrief workshops and presentations. A highly recommended option is a quarterly or semiannually home-delivered trifold pamphlet identifying strengths and opportunities, actions planned, and the reiteration of the commitment to become a preferred employer.

Potential-Employee Communication

Employer strengths and opportunities, actions planned, and the commitment to become a preferred employer can be an effective attraction and recruitment tool. Survey data and preferred employer commitment information can become collateral for website and recruitment advertising content, career centers, and website campaigns.

Public Relations and Popular Press Communications

Organizations can establish their employment brand as a preferred employer with earned positive media impressions, event placements, and influential podcasts. This can optimize discoverability and increase attraction, recruitment, and retention.

Preferred Employer Celebrations Communication

Celebration events, press releases of continued commitment to increasingly becoming a preferred employer, video clips of employees for the website, articles for popular press, case study white papers for professional press, and presentations at association meetings externally brand the organization as a preferred employer.

STEP 6: ONGOING COLLECTION AND EVALUATION OF THE EMPLOYEE VOICE

Data gathering continues concurrent with action to both measure and determine the effectiveness of any action, to feed the results to all organization members, *and* to continuously re-diagnose and determine additional location- and/or role-specific requirements.

Quo Vadis?

The Latin phrase meaning "Where are you going?" applies perfectly to today's retention and engagement struggle. Employee-centric needs assessment, evidence-based solutions, and evaluation measures are critical to successfully revising and executing a productivity strategy. Determining the costs of retention and engagement and understanding the real reasons why people come to the organization, why they stay, and why people would or wouldn't work for the organization again provide the necessary information to responsibly intervene, reduce human expense, and increase productivity.

STOP AND THINK

So, what about you? What are your plans?

Who is your organization, and where is it going?

Businesses will continue to compete for skilled workers for several years to come. To compete, grow, and win, employers must have workers with the skills and knowledge required to do the work that needs to get done. As the employees' market is likely to continue, an approach to compete and succeed needs to be more than cosmetically different from the competition's. Becoming an Engaged Employ-ER—a preferred employer—is a branding strategy that supports that differentiation.

In the following sections you will find: **"An Open Letter to HR Colleagues,"** written by Danny Nelms, president of the Work Institute. **Appendix A**, which is a compilation of the STOP AND THINK exercises throughout this book. You are encouraged to revisit these exercises periodically and take note of insightful shifts in your leadership or workforce perspective. **Appendix B**, which presents a summary case study of Renal Advantage, Inc. and their quantified return on investment by implementing the EmployER Engagement Model. These resources are designed to inform and guide you through your own approach to EmployER Engagement.

It's time to cross out that last E in your attraction and retention strategy. Insert the letter R.

AN OPEN LETTER TO HR COLLEAGUES

FROM DANNY NELMS, PRESIDENT OF THE WORK INSTITUTE

This is a great time for human resource, organization development, and learning professionals who want to secure and maintain a leadership role in their businesses—if they choose.

For as long as I can remember, human resource leaders have aspired to a seat at the big table, yet in most companies the seat is not offered. A seat at that table requires someone with confidence and bold awareness, with the combined knowledge and skill of a behavior scientist and a business practitioner, and a sense of urgency equal to the business leaders who are at the table.

In my role as a workforce and workplace behavior expert, I talk daily with human resource leaders about their challenges in attracting, retaining, and engaging their workforce. However, continuing to both fascinate and frustrate me is the lack of urgency in tackling this manageable challenge. I hear, "Follow up with me next quarter," or "I am so busy I can't do this now," or "We need to look at this at budget time." The need for urgency is real: companies are likely to lose one in four employees this year, as employees will seek employment elsewhere. When an employee quits, money walks out the door just as it does when a company or organization loses a customer. If companies were losing one in four of their customers, the entire company would be in panic mode and looking for solutions TODAY.

Too many companies continue to complain about losing key talent and dealing with a disengaged workforce while at the same time doing little to change it. Employers are not identifying and creating the necessary conditions wherein employees are most likely to engage in their work.

Human resource leaders can provide business intelligence to executive colleagues to help them better run their businesses. This includes providing workforce preference, expectation, and intent intelligence, and the financial consequence of NOT acting on the identified workforce preferences, expectations, and intents.

However, human resources must present business recommendations through a financial impact lens. Human resource recommendations and activities can drive business success by focusing on the human capital financials, attraction, and retention that make a difference.

Winning the talent war is what will keep companies growing and profitable. It is time for human resources to study, report, act, evaluate, and communicate—with urgency.

There is an opportunity.

Danny Nelms
President, Work Institute

Appendix A:
"Stop and Think" Exercises

STOP AND THINK

If you are a manager, think about your time as an employee; consider those days before you became a manager. What were your aspirations? What were your pressures and responsibilities inside the office? What were your pressures and responsibilities outside the office?

Were your aspirations and past experiences really any different from those of today's young employee? What might be done to make life just a bit easier?

If you are currently a nonmanagement employee, please attempt to look through the eyes of managers. Do their pressures and role expectations inside and outside the office differ from yours?

What might be done to make their lives just a bit easier?

STOP AND THINK

Thirty-eight percent of all turnover is attributed to employees who quit in their first year. What are the consequences of 38 percent of your product or service failing in the first year?

What percentage of your employees quit in the first year?

Of the more controllable reasons for leaving in 2018, those who quit within the first year cited work-life balance, career development, manager behavior, job characteristics, and work environment as the most important reasons for leaving.

But what about your organization? Why are employees quitting in the first year?

What are you doing to solve this?
(Hint: the solution is not to hire more recruiters.)

STOP AND THINK

Is it the employee or the employer who is disengaged? Is it both?

Where do you need to intervene?

With the employee?

With the employer?

With the workplace conditions?

STOP AND THINK

A manager's view of employees is sometimes shaped by assumptions about roles. The way we view our and others' roles and make judgements about them directs our behavior.

What do you believe is the difference between a manager perspective and an employee perspective?

Think of the differences on a day-to-day basis. How do a manager's beliefs affect an employee's overall engagement and intent to stay?

Consider this: They are not your employees. You are their employer.

Does this shift your thinking? How?

STOP AND THINK

What percentage of poor hiring decisions would be considered as unacceptable hiring performance?

What percentage of turnover would be acceptable?

How many sexual harassment claims are reasonable?

What percentage of the workforce intending to leave in the next quarter is acceptable?

STOP AND THINK

At Renal Advantage, Dean Weiland, COO, and Dr. Linda Meador, CHRO, attributed retention success to the fact that regional managers were held accountable for retention. Bonuses throughout were specifically tied to increased "excellent" ratings and reductions in turnover.

If your managers and supervisors were held accountable for engagement and retention, how might that change their behavior toward employees?

What would managers and supervisors do differently?

What might they stop doing?

What might they start doing?

STOP AND THINK

How about you? When do you plan to look for a new job? In the next thirty days, in the next ninety days, six months, two years, or not for a long time?

What would need to be different to increase your length of stay with your current employer?

What else? What else?

Of those reasons, which is the most important?

STOP AND THINK

Does that job description you are writing really require a degree? Why?

STOP AND THINK

Are you aware of any harmful, unethical, illegal, or financial impropriety within your organization?

STOP AND THINK

Who are you, and why are you here?

STOP AND THINK

Now, if I'm the CEO, what is my expectation?

If I am the chief revenue officer, what is my expectation?

If I am the chief human resource officer, what is my expectation?

STOP AND THINK

Consider what you could save if you made investments in the many other reasons people leave organizations.

Using the above provided numbers, what if 11 percent of your people (1,100) are quitting or intend to quit because of poor supervisory behavior. That is a cost of more than $16 million.

Is there an ROI to your organization by intervening to address poor manager communication, unprofessionalism, lack of support, or unfairness?

Mock up a calculation. And remember: savings all go to the bottom line.

STOP AND THINK

Accounting systems of the last seventy-five years were built on models relevant to a manufacturing economy. However, as we have changed from a manufacturing economy to a human behavior economy, generally accepted accounting practices require reinvention.

Some companies make good attempts at suggesting "employees are their greatest assets." However, as long as employees are on the liability side of the balance sheet, they are not an asset.

- Perhaps it is time to figure out how to move employees over to the asset side of the balance sheet.

- Perhaps it is time to recognize that on-time, on-skill, and on-task employees enhance their value.

- Perhaps it is time to recognize that on-time, on-skill, and on-task employees enhance the company's value.

STOP AND THINK

How would your company's climate improve if (1) you could identify reasons why employees left or intend to leave, and

(2) you acted on what you can do to increase length-of-stay?

STOP AND THINK

Reread the Preferred and Engaged EmployER Principles.

Are these core philosophical beliefs of yours already?

What about your organization?

What needs to happen for your organization to subscribe to these principles?

STOP AND THINK

How would your company improve if you could proactively identify behavioral, financial, ethical, and legal risks and respond before people, financials, brand, and safety are compromised?

STOP AND THINK

So, what about you? What are your plans?

Who is your organization, and where is it going?

APPENDIX B:
RAI CASE STUDY

The challenge: Renal Advantage Inc. (RAI) faced a predicted 20 percent gap in the supply and demand of nurses by 2020 and the knowledge that 17 percent of health-care workers were dissatisfied. They needed to figure out how to retain their employees and avoid high turnover.

The solution: the Work Institute conducted incumbent interviews to target three key areas of improvement—the perception of RAI as an employer, the quality of supervisor performance, and overall turnover.

The results:

- The number of people who rated RAI as an "excellent" employer increased by 22 percent.

- The number of people who rated their supervisor as "excellent" increased by 10 percent.

- The number of employees with an intent to leave within the first year at RAI decreased from 22 percent to 16 percent.

Founded by veteran health professionals, Renal Advantage Inc. is one of the nation's leading providers of dialysis services. With over 135 freestanding centers nationwide, and additional centers developing rapidly, RAI operates as a center-focused organization in order to provide the best experience for both their patients and health-care providers. Linda Meador, PhD, Vice President of Human Resources, emphasizes their commitment to employee satisfaction, saying, "We believe our employees are a primary customer."

RAI was formed with the purchase of seventy-three freestanding dialysis centers when two dialysis service providers, DaVita Inc. and Gambro Healthcare, merged. After the merger, RAI leadership was interested to see exactly how their employees were affected. Meador explains, "We wanted to be able to understand our employees' wants, needs, and their perception of the organization at that time. We needed to get a really good feel for how well we did with the integration of two very different companies."

Senior leadership at RAI recognized that, while they were not the largest provider of dialysis services in the United States, they were going to differentiate themselves as a preferred employer; therefore, their competitive advantage would be their workforce. RAI chose to focus on two major areas—supply/demand and attraction/retention. With an aging nursing population, a predicted 20 percent gap in the supply and demand of nurses by 2020, and the knowledge that 17 percent of health-care workers are dissatisfied, Dr. Meador and her team understood just how costly turnover can be.

To reduce costs associated with employee disengagement and turnover, RAI partnered with the Work Institute to conduct a baseline survey with their entire employee population. RAI needed to know the preferences, expectations, and intents of their workforce. Keeping their finger on the pulse of the workforce provides the organization with the opportunity to address disengagement before employees walk out the door.

RAI focused on three key areas for improvement: the perception of RAI as an employer, the quality of supervisor performance, and overall turnover. For both the perception of RAI as an employer and the quality of supervisor performance, all supervisors were responsible for driving the percent of "fair"/"poor" responses below 15 percent, and the percent of "excellent" responses above 30 percent. As an organization, Renal Advantage endeavored to have the total "intent to leave within one year" be less than 15 percent. The human resources department at RAI served as the key driver of this process. With the support of the executive management team, HR worked with the Work Institute to develop the questionnaire. To maximize RAI's ability to set targets and measure the progress toward their goals, a five-point-rating-scale question design (excellent, very good, good, fair, and poor) was used. Follow-up questions, such as "Why?" and "What would it take to get an "excellent" rating?" allowed interviewers to follow up with employees for more detailed information. The qualitative data provided the organization with actionable data that drove evidence-based decisions to earn employees' highest endorsement.

In February 2006, the Work Institute surveyed the entire workforce to gather baseline data, and goals were set based on the initial results. Then, in October 2006, the Work Institute interviewed 50 percent of the workforce to begin the biannual pulse surveys. Once the two data points had been collected and analyzed, in early 2007, Meador and Christie Carlisle, Director of Human Resources, traveled to each RAI region to equip supervisors with the tools and techniques to build and execute action plans.

Following the initial training and goal-setting, supervisors had three months to evaluate their own data and present action plans to their center and regional directors. The quantitative rating scores, coupled with verbatim responses, allowed each supervisor to gain a robust understanding of his or her strengths, weaknesses, and opportunities for improvement. By the end of 2007, RAI's human resources team had evaluated all interventions and celebrated the success of the evidence-based action-planning initiative using data obtained from the employee pulse surveys.

Following the internal adjustments, employee pulse surveys indicate that satisfaction with RAI drastically increased between 2006 and 2008. The number of employees who rated their employer as "excellent" increased by 22 percent; the number of employees rating their supervisors as "excellent" improved by 10 percent; and the number of employees with an intent to leave within the first year at RAI decreased from 22 percent to 16 percent. RAI leadership came away "surprised that we were able to hit some of our targets so quickly."

In 2008, Renal Advantage Inc. was designated as a four-star Certified Preferred Employer (CPE) by the Work Institute as a result of their dedication to continuous improvement. CPE is a brand that ensures employees, both current and potential, that RAI is constantly striving to better their employer-employee relationship. They have found the brand to be a beneficial marketing tool, noting that "it is something we can market, and a good way to recruit employees." RAI and the Work Institute refresh data with employee pulse surveys every six months.

*Note: Fresenius Medical Care purchased Renal Advantage Inc. in 2011.

Made in the USA
Middletown, DE
16 January 2020